Complete
Confectionery
Techniques

Complete
Confectionery
Techniques

Ildo Nicolello and Rowland Foote

Foreword by Michael Nadell

Hodder & Stoughton

A MEMBER OF THE HODDER HEADLINE GROUP

British Library Cataloguing in Publication Data

Nicolello, I.
  Complete Confectionery Techniques
  I. Title   II. Foote, Rowland
  641.86

ISBN 0 340 58259 6

First published 1994
Impression number 10 9 8 7 6 5 4 3 2 1
Year   1999 1998 1997 1996 1995 1994

Typeset by Wearset, Boldon, Tyne and Wear.
Printed in Hong Kong for Hodder & Stoughton Educational,
a division of Hodder Headline Plc, 338 Euston Road,
London NW1 3BH by Colorcraft Ltd.

CONTENTS

FOREWORD

I have been a pastry chef for many years now, having chosen to specialise in pâtisserie shortly after completing my training at Westminster School of Catering. At that time I was also drawn towards the fish and sauce sections, but pâtisserie won me over. Looking back, I realise my choice has brought me great reward – the years seem to have sped swiftly by, filled with happiness in my craft and a real sense of achievement. The magic and enthusiasm is still there as strong as ever, and I am never happier than when working with sugar, which is a great love of mine. I have never become bored in my work because, even if one creates something very good today, there is always the excitement of believing that tomorrow's effort will achieve a masterpiece.

Throughout my career I have been an avid collector of books relating to our industry, particularly, of course, those featuring pâtisserie, many of which I have read and used constantly in relation to my work. It is also a form of relaxation and enjoyment for me.

Upon reading *Complete Confectionery Techniques* I was extremely impressed by the depth in which each subject was covered – from basic raw materials to finished piece. It was obvious that this book had been put together in a most thorough and meticulous manner – unlike many others which just skim over the surface. I particularly liked the down-to-earth, straightforward style of addressing the reader – such information will be much appreciated by students and will be of great benefit in increasing their understanding of both their craft and the materials involved.

This book is full of recipes that really work and it will be a continuing asset not only to the advanced pastry student, but also to chefs who wish to learn about the advanced techniques of pâtisserie.

I am confident that *Complete Confectionery Techniques* will become *the* manual to all aspiring students of advanced pâtisserie.

From myself, and on behalf of all the future readers of this book, my congratulations and thanks go to Ildo Nicolello and Rowland Foote for the time and effort spent in compiling this excellent book. Best wishes to you both.

Michael Nadell
(of Nadell Pâtisserie)

PREFACE

Ildo Nicolello, FEWMCS, ACF, NCFA (CG)
Cordon Culinaire Lacam

In writing this companion book to *Complete Pastrywork Techniques*, my aim was again to advise and inspire both students and professional pâtissiers, chefs and bakers.

The book will be valuable to those working towards competence at NVQ level 3. It is specifically structured to assist the student with each relevant unit, and provides specific information related to the performance criteria and underpinning knowledge.

The text will also be an essential resource for the workplace, providing practical information on confectionery techniques. Whether you are a student or experienced confectioner, this book will enable you to discover the fascinating and absorbing art of confectionery.

I owe a great debt of gratitude to my friend and colleague, Rowland Foote, for his help in writing the Marzipan and Chocolate chapters of this book, and for his contributions to the section on friandises. His guidance in the execution of my work has been indispensable.

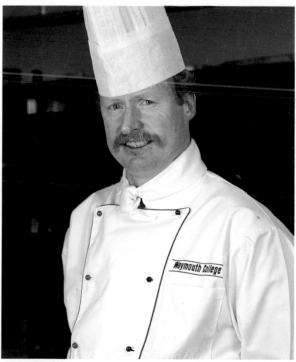

Rowland Foote, BEd (Hons), Cert-Ed, ACF, LCG

Our culture is re-appraising the lost quality in food and we are re-visiting the basics, seeking to promote the apprentice, pupil and trainee philosopher of confectionery and pâtisserie. I, myself, was so fortunate to gain experience with Adamson, Simmonds, Jannaway and others.

I am honoured and humbled by the knowledge and enthusiasm, the depth and artistry of Ildo Nicolello. In helping to write this book, I hope I do justice to those who have trained but not been teachers, to those who have toiled but not been recognised, to those who have suffered the pressures of catering yet have no medal or glory. It is to these that I dedicate this book and hope that others will develop the passion and dedication to detail which have given me so much satisfaction and pleasure in my work.

ACKNOWLEDGEMENTS

The authors wish to thank their colleges for supplying ingredients used in the photographs and providing permission to use the facilities – particularly Gian Paolo Fanchini, Associate Dean of West Herts College and Don Brierley, Principal of Weymouth College. Thanks also to Ian Bligh for his enthusiastic assistance and help, and to Rod Naylor of Exeter College for advice on moulds. Special thanks go to the assistant, Lee Gardner, for his help in preparing the dishes. The photographs were taken by Roddy Paine and his assistant, David Barnes – we are grateful to them for their time and co-operation.

We are also grateful to the following for providing assistance, materials and equipment for this book:

Mr Alan Booth of Cadbury Ltd
Bournville Lane
Bournville
Birmingham
B30 2LV

Mr Graham Beaumont and Mr Toby King
Ritter Courivaud Ltd
17 Northfield Industrial Estate
Beresford Avenue
Wembley
Middlesex
HA0 1GJ
Tel: 081 903 7177/8/9

S&A Lesme-Callebaut Ltd
Banbury
Oxfordshire
OX16 7UU
Tel: 0295 257651

J.F. Renshaw Ltd
Mitcham House
River Court
Albert Drive
Woking
Surrey
GU21 5RP
Tel: 0483 776070

PME Sugar Craft Supplies
Brember Road
South Harrow
Middlesex
HA2 8UN
Tel: 081 864 0888

Keylink Ltd
Blackburn Road
Rotherham
S61 2DR
Tel: 0709 550206

ABPAC Bakery Supplies
ABPAC House
Wessex Way
Wincanton
Somerset
BA9 9RR
0963 32913

CFO (Cake Artistry Supplies)
Unit 26a
Granby Industrial Estate
Cambridge Road
Weymouth
Tel: 0305 772922

INTRODUCTION

A selection of sugars (left to right from back: caster sugar, black treacle, foot sugar, cube sugar, honey, muscovado sugar, icing sugar, demerera sugar, granulated sugar, sugar crystals, cubed demerera sugar, nibbed sugar, golden syrup)

SUGAR

Sugar is a natural substance occurring in two plants: cane and beet.

Sugar cane is an enormous grass, growing as high as 5–6 metres, which requires tropical or sub-tropical temperatures and plenty of rain. The main countries producing cane sugar are India, Java, Cuba, Hawaii, Japan, Brazil and the USA. It is usually harvested before the crop is fully matured, so that it can be processed before it has passed its optimum condition. The cut cane is processed as soon as possible after harvesting.

Sugar beet is an extremely profitable crop which is cultivated mostly in Germany, Russia, the USA and France. A large quantity is also grown in the UK. The beets are transported to a factory, where the roots are cut into thin slices. The sugar is then removed by soaking these in warm water. Several such soaking treatments are required to remove all the sugar from the pulp. It is then filtered to remove impurities. The final stages in the extraction of refined sugar closely follow the processes in the manufacture of cane sugar, as shown below.

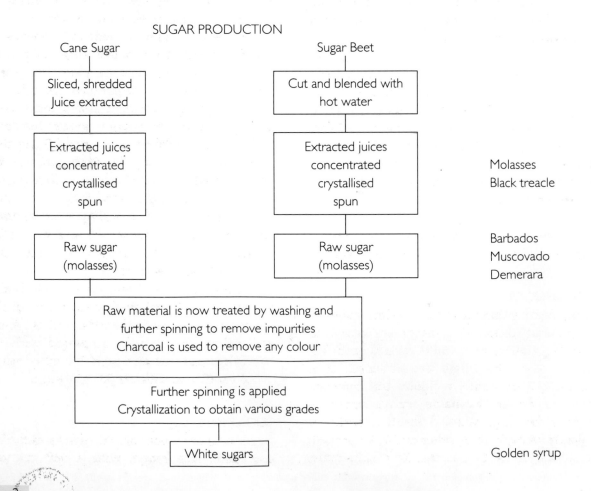

White sugars or refined sugar

WHITE CASTER AND GRANULATED SUGARS

Caster and granulated sugars are made by first boiling the liquid sugar syrup in vacuum pans, as rapidly as possible, until crystals are formed. The mixture is then fed into centrifugal machines which spin off the crystals. Any remaining moisture is extracted by the use of granulators, large rotating drums into which warm filtered air is drawn. The dry crystals are then conveyed to another machine which sorts the crystals into various grades according to size. Granulated sugar is one of a range of large sugar crystals. Caster sugar has smaller crystals.

These are high quality sugars which are free flowing, have a low level of foaming when boiled and contain a pure source of fermentable carbohydrate.

Granulated sugar is the most versatile type, suitable for fondant manufacturing, boiled sugar work, boiled sweets, jams and marmalades. It acts as a sweetening agent in beers, ciders and wines. It is also essential for biscuit manufacture, providing the correct texture and also contributing to the uniformity of size in the final product.

Caster sugar is useful in confectionery, creaming, mixtures, pastes, whisking and batters.

ICING SUGAR

Icing sugar is prepared by grinding cubes of granulated sugar, using machinery known as disintegrators or mills, until various grades of fine or semi-fine sugar are obtained. It is generally very white in colour, but coloured icing sugars are available with a superfine texture for icing cakes. A small quantity of calcium phosphate or other anti-caking agent is added to assist its free-flowing texture, prevent lumps forming and absorb any moisture.

Icing sugar is an ideal ingredient for the production of royal and other icings, butter creams, biscuits, and confectionery fondants and pastes.

CUBE SUGAR

As far back as medieval times, large lumps of sugar were given names like sugar stone, sugar loaf and sugar rock. In later years loaves of sugar were made by running the syrup into conical-shaped iron frames, leaving a hole in the tip for the syrup to drain away. The mould was eventually removed and the cone-shaped sugar was placed in a warm room to dry. Cube sugar was originally obtained by cutting the sugar loaf, using saw blades or sheets of cutters arranged to work on a machine.

Cube sugar is now made in two ways. In the first method the boiled sugar is poured straight from the vacuum pans into small compartments of a segmented mould. The mould segments are then assembled, cooled and spun in a centrifugal machine; the small slabs of sugar formed in the moulds are then dried and cut into regular-sized cubes. In the second method, boiled sugar is first passed through centrifugal machines and then pressed into cube or other shapes before being dried and cut if desired. These are called pressed sugar cubes (quick-dissolving cubes are compressed less firmly).

Cube sugar is mainly used for boiled sweets, jam-making, stock syrups, confits and sauces. Cube sugar is the most suitable sugar for boiling as it can be saturated with the minimum amount of water: 100 ml of water would suffice to saturate 500 g of sugar.

SUGAR NIBS

Sugar nibs are pieces of loaf sugar screened to a particle size range, with a soft crunchy texture. They are mainly used for sprinkling on cakes, sweet buns and chocolate confectionery.

Brown sugars or unrefined sugar

These sugars are unrefined, moist to the touch, and adhere in lumps owing to the relatively large quantity of syrup present (known as cane molasses).

Raw sugars possess a characteristic flavour in addition to sweetness, due mainly to aromatic substances in the large amount of molasses present. Brown sugars have the aroma, rich flavour and colour that is always associated with raw cane sugar. They are used widely in health products, confectionery and baked goods, giving a distinctive, characteristic flavour and aroma to the finished confection. Brown sugars are particularly suitable for the manufacture of rich fruit cakes, puddings, and confectionery such as toffee and fudge.

FOOT SUGAR

This is crude, unrefined or raw sugar, which is very dark brown in colour and contains a considerable amount of molasses and uncrystallised sugar. The name originates from the time when Barbados sugar was imported in hogsheads (large casks). The molasses, which had not been completely cleared from the crude sugar, settled at the bottom of the hogshead. This layer, which was much darker and very moist, was given the name 'foot sugar'.

Foot sugar is ideal for dark cakes, such as wedding, birthday, Christmas cakes, etc. It is particularly good in Christmas puddings.

BARBADOS OR MUSCOVADO SUGAR

This partly purified sugar is imported from Barbados. Dark brown to reddish in colour, with a rich flavour, it may be blended with other sugars to impart its characteristics to the finished confection. Its main uses are in sauces, boiled sweets, rich fruit cakes and puddings.

DEMERARA

This is a partly purified crystalline sugar imported from the British Guyana colony of Demerara. It consists of yellowish crystals with a pleasant syrupy flavour, making it suitable for domestic use. It is used for some boiled sweets, toffees and fudge.

MOLASSES

This is the residual syrup left when sugar has been through the crystallisation process and no more crystals of sucrose can be economically obtained. The molasses from cane sugar is an edible product, but that from raw beet sugar has a stronger, bitter taste and is mainly used in the production of cattle food, as it contains a useful amount of calcium and iron.

Molasses from cane sugar is widely used for fermenting in the manufacture of rum or other spirits. Mixed molasses are also used in the manufacture of yeast.

BLACK TREACLE

This dark viscous syrup is one of the by-products in the refining of sugar. It is the liquid portion which drains from the sugar crystals in the crystallising vats. It possesses a unique flavour and is used in many sectors of industry not only for its flavour, but also to provide colour. In the baking trade it is particularly useful in the production of Christmas produce, and is used either alone or with a proportion of milk or water for gingerbread, gingernuts and parkin.

GOLDEN SYRUP

This golden-coloured viscous syrup has a unique flavour. It is resistant to crystallisation and has many industrial applications, being used for flavour in bakery and confectionery work. It is made by partially inverting syrup taken from the sugar refining process. It is very soluble in water and stable solutions of high concentrations are used in jam and preserve manufacture where the concentrated solution acts as an effective preservative. Invert sugar in baked products helps with moisture retention and can improve keeping properties. Golden syrup is classified as a pure sugar product.

Honey

Honey is a golden sugary fluid, made by bees and other insects from nectar collected from flowers. It has many uses. A glass of hot water with honey, lemon and whisky will calm a sore throat and guarantee a quiet night. Experts have discovered that honey helps to build up the strength of babies who cannot readily take other forms of sugar. Nutritionists regard honey as a veritable powerhouse of energy, for there is probably no other naturally occurring food which can raise the blood sugar count so rapidly.

The earliest confectioners made good use of honey, and even today certain traditional sweets such as nougat and marshmallow are based on honey. Honey contains an average of about 75% invert sugar and is therefore noticeably hygroscopic. Its main use in confectionery is to impart its distinctive flavour.

Glucose

Glucose syrup is a colourless, viscous fluid, principally made from starchy foods such as maize, potatoes and wheat. It is produced by mixing starch, water and a small amount of sulphuric acid. When the starch has hydrolysed, the mixture no longer turns blue when tested with iodine. Chalk is added to the solution, the acid is neutralised and the insoluble salts are allowed to settle. The upper liquid is separated and concentrated to the consistency of a syrup, comprised of dextrose, maltose and dextrins. Liquid glucose is a very important basic ingredient in confectionery because it does not crystallise and, when mixed with a sugar solution, it tends to prevent the sugar from crystallising.

Glucose is hygroscopic – it absorbs moisture from the air. Therefore, in sweet-making for example, products containing glucose will remain moist. The confectioner has a wide range of uses for liquid glucose: in chocolate, marzipan and many other confectionery products.

COLOURING FOR CONFECTIONERY

As far back as Roman times colouring was added to breads and wines, using either white earth (chalk soil) or berries. Colouring is primarily used in confectionery to improve its appearance (or to restore its original appearance) and also to obtain a consistent appearance between batches of foods.

The prime objective when using colourings in food and items connected with food is that it should have an edible appearance. Most food colours are acceptable for this purpose, except blue which is considered unsuitable by most confectioners.

Certain colours complement each other, depending on two factors:

1 The light available to view the object.
2 A person's ability to perceive and respond to colours.

Each primary colour is always complemented by the secondary colour lying directly opposite on the colour wheel (see page 7).

Food colours have attracted a great deal of controversy, partly because they are cos-

5

metic and partly because of the connection between some artificial dyes and allergic reactions to food. The use of colouring agents is strictly regulated by the European Community as well as the UK. All permitted colours have a number, though not all have been allocated an 'E' prefix. Colours are numbered within the range E100–E199. The regulations do not, however, distinguish between colours of natural and synthetic origin.

which azo dyes form the main group. They include:

Tartrazine (E102)
Amaranth (E123)
Sunset yellow (E110)
Ponceau 4R (E124)
Carmoisine (E122)
Black PN (E151)

Types of colouring

NATURAL
These lack stability and mainly come from pigments extracted from plant and animal tissues, including:

Chlorophyll: The green pigment contained in the leaves and stems of plants.

Carotenoid: Yellow to orange-red colours which are found in abundance in apricots, carrots, oranges, corn, peaches, tomatoes, and in the skins of bananas.

Anthocyanin: Red, blue and violet pigments found in beetroot, plums, raspberries, red cabbage and black grapes.

Flavone: Yellow pigment that can be found in the leaves and petals of almost every plant.

Sugar: When heat treated, a chemical reaction occurs, leading to the brown found in caramel.

SYNTHETIC COLOURS
These can cause hyperactivity and other allergic reactions, so they are strictly controlled. Twenty synthetic colours are permitted, of

Permitted food colourings

There are 58 permitted colours, including 20 permitted artificial colours. The following list gives some of these permitted colourings.

E100	Curcumin
E102	Tartrazine
E104	Quinoline yellow
E110	Sunset yellow
E120	Cochineal
E122	Carmoisine
E123	Amaranth
E124	Ponceau 4R
E127	Erythrosine
128	Red 2G
E132	Indigo carmine
133	Brilliant blue
E140	Chlorophyll
E141	Copper complex of chlorophyll
142	Green S
E150	Caramel
E153	Carbon black
	Vegetable brown
154	Brown FK
155	Chocolate brown HT
E160(a–f)	Carotenoids
E162	Betamin (Beetroot red)
	Paprika extract
	Saffron
	Sandalwood

Choosing and using colour

COLOUR WHEEL
The colour wheel is an idea, meant to be used as a guide not a scientific tool. You can make a wheel with any medium, using food colouring pastes, liquids or dusting powders applied with a brush, sponge or spray. Remember, the colours you put in will never have the rainbow purity of the spectrum.

PRIMARY COLOURS
Red, blue and yellow are the three colours

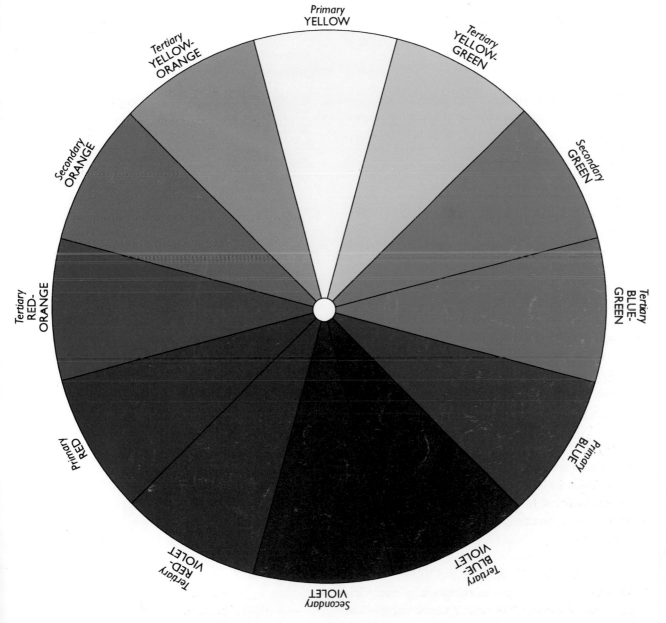

Colour wheel

which form the basis of all other colours. Black and white also have significance in confectionery, but are mainly used for finishing off specific items, giving a realistic touch to flowers, lettering, figures, plaques, and any non-edible or removable items.

SECONDARY COLOURS

These are obtained by mixing two primaries. Orange is mixed from red and yellow, green from yellow and blue, and violet from red and blue.

TERTIARY COLOURS

Red-orange, yellow-green and violet-blue are made by mixing a primary and a secondary colour.

CLOSELY RELATED COLOURS

These are next to each other on the colour wheel. They share a common base colour – for example, yellow-orange, orange and red-orange all have the colour orange in common; blue-green, blue and blue-violet all have blue in common.

COMPLEMENTARY COLOURS

Complementary colours lie exactly opposite on the colour wheel. Notice that each primary colour is always complemented by a secondary colour – it is never opposite another primary.

TEMPERATURE

Some colours look warm, others look cool. Divide the colour wheel down the middle, splitting yellow at the top and violet at the bottom. You can see on the left side that the reds and oranges are warm and vibrant, and on the right side the greens and blues are cool and calming. But what about yellow and violet? The yellow section on the orange side looks warm, while the yellow section on the green side looks cool. Violet is warmer towards red and cooler towards blue.

ADJUSTING AND MIXING COLOURS

When adjusting colours, it is important to work your way gradually towards a solution, like descending a ladder rather than jumping off a roof. In confectionery, white icing is generally the prominent base colour – start by adding a closely related colour.

Chocolate can be obtained by mixing an equal amount of orange and green.

Coffee is made by mixing equal quantities of green and orange.

Peach can be obtained by gradually adding red to yellow until the correct shade is reached.

Apricot can also be obtained by gradually adding yellow to red until the correct shade is reached.

■ FLAVOURING SUBSTANCES

When preparing confectionery, almost all flavours are permitted, particularly for moistening sponges. Blended flavours can give good results, and all the well-known liqueurs may be used on the strict condition that they are blended with at least one-third of strong stock syrup, fruit syrup or juice.

Flavouring and extracts are classified under three categories:

1 Natural origin, for example those consisting of essential oils, fruit juices, herbs and root extract.
2 Synthetic origin, for example those consisting of esters (organic compounds), acids, alcohols, etc.
3 Blend of natural and synthetic products.

The use of flavours in confectionery work is not intended to disguise inferior ingredients, such as rancid fats or stale eggs.

The aim of a skilful confectioner will always be to achieve the perfect texture and appearance. However, all labour will have been in vain if the flavours have been badly chosen. Badly flavoured products are as harmful to the reputation as less skilfully prepared articles which appeal to the palate.

The usual flavourings for confectionery work are vanilla, lemon, almond, strawberry, raspberry, maraschino, peppermint, cherry, apricot, pear, lime, banana, pineapple, orange, orange flower water, rose flower water, chocolate and coffee.

Essential oils from fruits, herbs and spices are obtained from practically every part of the plant: fruit, flower, seed, leaf, wood and root. Typical examples of flavouring oils are anise, caraway, cassia, cinnamon, clove, coriander, nutmeg, peppermint, orange and rose flower. Separation of these oils is accomplished by treatment with steam. The vapour of oil and water rises, condenses and separates in two layers, with the oils either floating or sinking depending on the specific gravity. Orange flower and rose petal water are used in the production of marshmallows and Turkish delight. Oils from lemons, oranges and mandarins are obtained by means of strong pressure upon the rinds, which ruptures the oil cells; the oil then escapes and is collected on the surface of the water. Vanilla beans are the fruits of the orchid *Vanilla planifolia*, grown in Mexico, Seychelles, Java, Singapore, Ceylon and some parts of Africa. The beans are collected and put through a curing process, necessary for the development of flavour.

To be able to assess the merits of different types of flavours, you have to understand the principles of flavour perception. Flavours can be divided into two main categories: the first includes those registered by the taste buds of the tongue and palate, which respond to such qualities as saltiness, sweetness, sourness and bitterness; the second consists of aromatic flavours such as those originating from fruits and flowers. The combined effects of taste and aroma produce the whole sensation known as flavour. Emphasis needs to be laid on measuring flavours. Each batch should have exactly the same amount of flavour as the preceding and subsequent batches.

To preserve the quality of essential oils, flavours and essences should be kept in tightly corked bottles to prevent loss via evaporation. The bottles should be stored in a cool place away from direct sunlight.

EQUIPMENT USED

This includes a brief description of the function of essential items used in the basic sugar studio.

ESSENTIAL EQUIPMENT

Marble slab	Container for oil
Copper saucepan	Container for water
Palette knives	Large knife
Metal scraper	Saucepan stand
Heated lamp	Basket frame
Blowing tube	Scissors
Thermometer	Gloves
Brushes	Old knives
Tea towels	Saucepans
Basin for cold water	Brush
Fan	Eye dropper
Blowing lamp	Oil lamp
Hair drier	Leaf mould
Blowing tube	Blowing pump
Alcohol burner	Moulds for sugar pouring

Saucepan: A specially manufactured copper saucepan is recommended. Most confectioners prefer it as copper is a good conductor of heat, and being a non-absorbent metal, it does not absorb grease. The lip of this saucepan also prevents hot sugar from flowing down the outside of the saucepan while pouring. It is important to clean these saucepans thoroughly just before needed with salt and acids such as vinegar. They can also be cleaned with a paste made from $\frac{1}{3}$ silver sand, $\frac{1}{3}$ salt and $\frac{1}{3}$ flour, mixed to a paste with vinegar. The saucepans are then thoroughly rinsed and dried.

Alternatively, a good quality stainless-steel saucepan, with a specially constructed heat-conductive bottom, allows the sugar to cook quickly and uniformly.

Sugar thermometer: This specially constructed thermometer is used to gauge the temperature of the syrup during the cooking process. Changes in barometric pressure and the position above sea level will effect the performance of a sugar or jam thermometer. To find a true reading, boil water for 5 minutes with the thermometer in place. If the water boils at 97°C, add three degrees to the final cooking temperature of the sugar. Alternatively, subtract three degrees from the final cooking temperature if the water boils at 103°C.

Pastry brush: A natural pastry brush should be used to remove the droplets of syrup that escape from the surface in the early stages of the cooking process and adhere to the lip and inside wall of the saucepan. Do not use dyed bristle brushes and never use a synthetic bristle brush. It is advisable to keep a brush purely for this purpose. New brushes should be soaked in cold water overnight.

Stainless steel strainer: A stainless steel strainer is used to remove the residue of mineral salts that appears on the surface of the syrup at the onset of rapid boil.

Eye dropper: A small glass eye dropper is used to add the tartaric acid and water mixture to the syrup in the final stages of the cooking process.

Marble slab: Essential for sugar boiling, this should be made of genuine, good quality marble. White tight-seamed marble is recommended, at least 2 cm thick (in actual fact, the thicker the marble the easier it is to handle the boiled sugar). The marble absorbs the heat and allows the sugar to cool slowly and uniformly. It should always be lightly oiled, using vegetable oil (some confectioners prefer to use liquid paraffin, as it is less greasy than oil). Always oil the marble using a soft tissue. Avoid scratching, marking or damaging the marble, as the sugar work will easily stick and give serious problems.

Airtight enclosure: Any container that can be rendered airtight can be used to store cooked sugar, either un-used bulk or completed items. Clear plastic freezer storage bags or plastic refrigerator containers would serve the purpose. Items made from sugar should be protected from moist atmospheric conditions, even for a short period. Specially produced, hermetically-sealed cabinets, made from glass or perspex, are essential for storage and for presentation of completed centrepieces to be placed on display. The cabinet should be made with a false perforated bottom containing silicate or quicklime which are very hygroscopic substances (i.e. they abstract moisture from the air). The lime decomposes quickly, so it must be changed regularly.

Bulb heating system: Standard 250-watt infrared bulbs, made with either red or white glass, are used to keep the cooked sugar warm and malleable, and to maintain the sugar-working temperature safely while work is in progres. If a dimmer could also be fitted, it would be advantageous for the control of temperature.

A thermostatically controlled hot-plate placed under the heating bulb also helps to maintain the sugar temperature. Alternatively, a fabric work rack can also serve as the working surface under the bulb. The white fabric, 100% polyester or silicon material, can be stretched tightly and stapled over a wooden frame to provide a firm working surface.

Blowing tubes: A standard blowpipe, made from either pyrex, glass or even the shell container of a ballpoint pen, will suffice for blowing sugar. The sizes can range from 6–10 mm in diameter. The size is determined by the size of the piece of sugar being blown. As the piece of sugar increases in size, so should the diameter of the blowing tube. Alternatively, hand and foot operated sugar-blowing pumps are on the market, specially produced for the purpose; in some cases they help the manipulation of the sugar, giving better results.

Alcohol burner: The alcohol burner uses methyl alcohol and produces a clean carbonless flame. The primary purpose of the alcohol burner is to supply the heating source required to weld the sugar.

Fan: The fan is useful for cooling the sugar when assembling and welding the pieces together, and for cooling the sugar while blowing. As the correct size and shape is reached, the fan will help to arrest any further movement.

Knives: Old, solid and pointed knives are extremely useful for cutting the sugar, where necessary. The knife can be heated over a small flame, then used gently. It can also be an efficient method of removing the blowing tube from a finished sugar-blown piece. The knives must not be over-heated, as this would cause discoloration of the completed pieces and spoil the appearance.

Scissors: A pair of good strong scissors are very useful to have ready for trimming particles of sugar and for dividing the bulk sugar kept warm under the lamp. Scissors must not be allowed to warm while working, as they will stick to the sugar and cause inconvenience in the manipulation of the work.

Basket frame: Use a wooden base, either round, oval or square, with holes the thickness of a pencil drilled around the edge – there should be an uneven number of holes. The pegs (10–15 cm) can be made from either metal nails or wooden dowels. They should fit in the holes comfortably, not too loose or too tight.

Hair drier: This is not essential, but is a useful piece of equipment to have around when sugar-boiling work is in progress. It should have a choice of settings for hot and cold air. The hair drier helps to selectively cool items of sugar where some parts have to be cooled and other parts have to remain warm.

SUGAR

■ SUGAR AND SUGAR SCIENCE

Solutions

A solution can be defined as a homogeneous mixture consisting of two or more substances; such solutions are called 'aqueous solutions' (from the Latin *aqua* meaning water). The liquid forming the solution is called the 'solvent'; the matter dissolved is referred to as the 'solute'.

A quantity of solids can be absorbed in a liquid without increasing its bulk; but it necessarily increases the weight for any given volume, which is called 'increasing the density'. Solid matter in solution in a liquid also raises the boiling point of the latter, and reduces the freezing point.

The solubility of a liquid increases with the temperature. When a liquid will dissolve no more of a substance at a certain temperature, but becomes more or less opaque, it is then considered as saturated.

Under certain conditions it is possible to supersaturate a liquid, i.e. to dissolve more sugar in it without producing a deposit; this means that there is more sugar dissolved in the solution than it can normally hold at a particular temperature. The supersaturated solution forms crystals – any addition of grease or other foreign matter will be sufficient to spark a formation chain of crystals.

BASIC TECHNIQUES
There are two basic techniques for producing solutions:

Dissolving salt or sugar in water.

Melting a solid to a liquid under the influence of heat.

WATER
Pure water is a compound liquid without colour, smell or taste. It is neutral, that is, neither acid nor alkaline. At ordinary atmospheric pressure water boils – is converted to the gaseous state or steam – at 100°C. However, it boils at a lower temperature under less pressure and at a higher temperature under greater pressure (as in the tubes of a steam pipe, for example, in steam ovens).

If a drop of water is thrown over highly heated sugar or on a highly heated plate, the drop becomes round and does not appear to boil, but gradually dries up. This is called its 'spheroidal' state. The appearance is due to a film of water vapour forming between the water and the heated surface.

FREEZING POINT AND BOILING POINT OF AQUEOUS SOLUTIONS
The freezing point of pure water is 0°C and its boiling point is 100°C when atmospheric pressure is normal. The presence of dissolved substances alters both of these properties.

The freezing point of a solution is lowered as the concentration of solute increases. Advantage is taken of this effect when we add glycerol to the water in the radiator of a car. The presence of the dissolved glycerol lowers the freezing point. In a similar way, we can use a mixture of salt and melting ice as a freezing mixture when making ice-cream.

On the other hand, the boiling point of a solution is raised as the concentration of solute increases. A practical application of this is used in sugar boiling and in jam boiling, when a sugar solution is boiled to a particular temperature. In this case the temperature is a measure of the sugar concentration.

CRYSTALLISATION

The molecules of the solute are dispersed in forming a solution, but as evaporation progresses the molecules of the solute come closer and closer together, until eventually they are sufficiently close to absorb one another and crystals are formed in a solid, crystalline, structural mass.

Sugar and sugar products

Sugar is a generic term applied to sugars from sugar cane, sugar beet and other vegetable juices. As a class, sugars are crystallisable and readily soluble in water, but less soluble or wholly insoluble in alcohol.

Sugar boiling equipment

Carbohydrates are important for our diet and are divided into two classes: those that are sweet and readily crystallisable, such as sugars, and those that are not crystallisable, such as starch and cellulose. Chemically, sugars contain active aldehyde or active ketone groups, which have the property of reducing alkaline copper solutions. In some sugars, however, these active groups are masked. Sugars may therefore be divided into reducing sugars, such as the monosaccharides arabinose, dextrose, laevulose, galactose and mannose and the disaccharides maltose, and non-reducing sugars, such as the disaccharides sucrose and the trisaccharides raffinose.

■ SUGAR BOILING

Sugar work is considered one of the most artistic aspects of confectionery work. Most skilled boiled sugar displays require an array of difficult techniques but, with good guidance and perseverance, these can be learned.

Sugar (sucrose) is a disaccharide which dissolves in about half its own weight of water. Its solubility increases as the temperature rises. By prolonging the boiling, moisture is evaporated and the viscosity of the sugar increases.

On hydrolysis the sugar undergoes a physical change and the two-molecule structure breaks into separate molecules – glucose and fructose (monosaccharides). The mixture of the two is known as invert sugar. On heating, dissolved sugar has a tendency to revert to its original nature, that is to grain or crystallise. As the crystallisation may be too rapid for the required task, it is necessary to introduce an extra quantity of non-crystalline or invert sugar – glucose. Alternatively, the crystallised sugar can be turned into invert sugar by adding tartaric acid.

When introducing either glucose or tar-

COMPLETE CONFECTIONERY TECHNIQUES

taric acid, take care not to use too much – too large a percentage of either would result in the boiling solution refusing to grain at all.

Crystallised sugars, despite the introduction of glucose, quickly grain if worked or stirred; for best results do not agitate or disturb the crystals during the boiling process.

It is important to pay attention to the condition of the vessels used for boiling: copper is considered the best as it has a smooth surface, can be easily kept clean and is a good conductor of heat – very important for sugar boiling.

Certain stages of the boiling process can be checked, either by the use of a sugar boiling thermometer or by testing a little of the boiling solution in cold water.

Cube or granulated sugars are always preferred for boiling purposes. It is even better to use sugars from small packages, which are more likely to be free from impurities (500 g packets).

Stock syrup

Stock syrups are part of the confectioner's everyday advanced preparation and can be used for numerous purposes: base for ice creams, fruit salad, confits, soaking of savarins and fondant.

Syrup is prepared by boiling sugar, water and glucose to various densities, according to the temperature reached.

Ingredients	
Cube or granulated sugar	1 kg
Water	1 litre
Glucose	200 g

Bring all the ingredients to the boil and continue on low heat, occasionally removing any surface scum and any crystals forming on the sides of the vessel. An instrument called a saccharometer can be used for measuring the density or appropriate degrees Baumé (see page 15). The saccharometer is placed in the cooled liquid, standing upright; the scale marked in degrees reads how much of the liquid is displaced.

Hygiene and safety precautions

At this stage particular attention should be paid to safety precautions, and to the hygiene of the equipment and working surfaces. The confectioner must ensure that all utensils are used safely, and should conform with regulations regarding the working area, particularly regarding the floor condition and the type and quality of working surfaces and equipment. Remember, even the smallest amount of dirt or grease in the sugar boiling solution can eventually cause the solution to crystallise.

Basic recipe for sugar boiling

Ingredients	
Cube or granulated sugar	500 g
Water	100 ml
Glucose or	60 g
Tartaric acid	5 drops

Place the sugar and water in the copper sugar boiler (alternatively a good solid stainless steel boiler can be used). Place over the heat, and heat gently to boiling point. While the initial boiling is in progress, remove any scum that appears on the surface, using a small ladle. Add the glucose or tartaric acid.

Rapid cooking is now an important factor in obtaining satisfactory results. All the sugar crystals should be dissolved before the syrup begins to boil, as the lumps do not readily dissolve in the boiling sugar; this can also cause recrystallisation and graining. Very slow boiling changes the colour of the sugar, and for this reason the boiler should be set over a good heat so that it can boil rapidly. Another point to remember is that if you add more water than necessary, the sugar has to remain longer over the heat before the required temperature is reached, and this tends to spoil the colour. Wash down the sides of the saucepan occasionally with a pastry brush while boiling to prevent crystals forming.

As the sugar solution is heated, it undergoes certain physical changes. With practice, certain stages of boiling are easily identified. The confectioner also identifies these stages of boiling by the temperature on the sugar thermometer. When the required temperature is reached, remove the pan from the heat and dip the base in cold water for a few seconds to stop the cooking. Place the saucepan on a stand on the work surface and allow the bubbles to subside. Use as required.

Measuring temperature and density

TEMPERATURE

A sugar thermometer is generally used for testing the boiling sugar. The instrument is mounted on a metal frame, with the degrees printed on the frame, starting from the top end at 200°C and decreasing to 0°C.

For safety reasons the thermometer should be rinsed in hot water before being immersed in the boiling solution and placed in a container of hot water when removed. Many confectioners find the thermometer unreliable because of changes in barometric pressure. The following chart will serve as a guide for those who prefer an alternative to the thermometer.

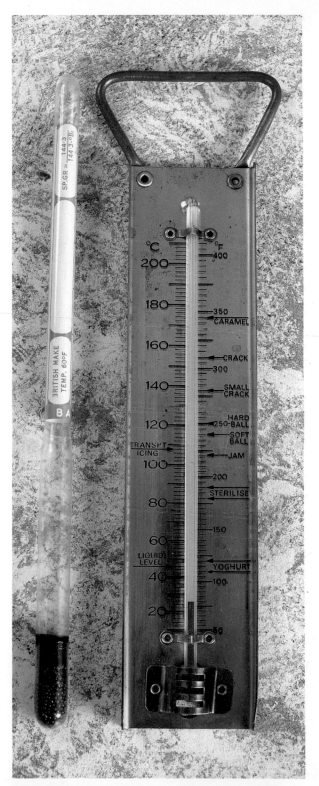

Sugar thermometer and saccharometer

TESTING FOR DEGREES

108°–112°C	Place a dry finger on the surface of the syrup, join together the finger and thumb and a thread should be formed. At this stage the sugar feels oily and contains 65% sucrose.
112°–115°C	Strong thread. At this stage the thread is thicker, with a viscous texture and a sucrose content of 83.5%.
118°C	Soft ball. The syrup sets into a soft ball shape. At this stage the solution tends to froth over and, if removed, may be blown into small feathery particles. The sugar content of the solution is 88.5%.
125°C	Hard ball. The syrup sets firmer. The sugar content solution is 88%.
140°C	Soft crack. The sugar will harden when immersed in water. The sugar content of the solution is 90%.
150°C	Crack. When cold, the sugar will break, crumbling. The sugar content is 95%.
155°C	Hard crack. When cold the sugar will crumble and will have a very slight amber tinge. The sugar content of the solution is about 98%. As boiling continues the sugar progressively darkens in colour and beyond 160°C will have the appearance of caramel.

Testing for degrees

Place a dry finger on the surface of the syrup

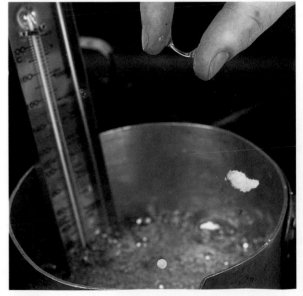

Thread

APPROPRIATE TEMPERATURES

Feather	115°C	Fondant, marzipan
Soft ball	118°C	Italian meringue
Hard ball	125°C	Italian meringue
Soft crack	140°C	Rock sugar, Italian meringue
Crack	148°C	Spun sugar, nougat montelimar, rock sugar, piped sugar, spun sugar
Hard crack	155°C	Glazed fruits, poured and pulled sugar, croquante, deguisés
Caramel	165°C	Caramel, dark nougat

Ball

Crack – the sugar should have an amber colour

A sugar solution boiled to 118°C crystallises to a hard granular mass on cooling. To prevent the formation of such crystals, or to 'cut the grain', the confectioner adds small quantities of an organic acid, such as tartaric acid, citric acid or cream of tartar, to the sugar solution. The acid causes slight inversion of the sucrose, and this invert sugar prevents the crystals forming, or at least delays their formation. By carefully regulating the amount of acid added and the boiling technique, subsequent crystal growth may be controlled.

THE DEVELOPMENT OF THERMOMETERS AND CALIBRATION

Scientists have developed various instruments for measuring temperature, particularly used by European Confectioners.

Anders Celsius (1701–1744), Swedish, invented the Centigrade thermometer.

Melting point of ice:	0
Boiling point of water:	100

Rene-Antoine Reaumur (1683–1757), French, invented the Reaumur thermometer.

Melting point of ice:	0
Boiling point of water:	80

Gabriel-Daniel Fahrenheit (1686–1736), Prussian, invented the Fahrenheit calibration.

Melting point of ice:	32
Boiling point of water:	212

CONVERSION CHART

Degrees may be converted from one scale into another as below:

D = Degrees   C = Centigrade
F = Fahrenheit   R = Reaumur

F into C	$(D - 32) \times 5/9$
F into R	$(D - 32) \times 4/9$
C into F	$(D \times 9/5) + 32$
R into F	$(D \times 9/4) + 32$
C into R	$D \times 4/5$
R into C	$D \times 5/4$

Fahrenheit	Centigrade	Reaumur	Fahrenheit	Centigrade	Reaumur
100	212	80.00	128.9	264	103.11
100.6	213	80.44	130.0	266	104.00
101.1	214	80.88	131.1	268	104.88
101.7	215	81.33	132.3	270	105.77
102.2	216	81.77	133.3	272	106.66
102.8	217	82.22	134.4	274	107.55
103.3	218	82.66	135.0	275	108.00
103.9	219	83.11	135.6	276	108.44
104.4	220	83.55	136.7	278	109.33
105.0	221	84.00	137.8	280	110.22
105.6	222	84.44	138.9	282	111.11
106.7	224	85.33	140.0	284	112.00
107.8	226	86.22	141.1	286	112.88
108.9	228	87.11	142.2	288	113.77
110.0	230	88.00	143.3	290	114.66
111.1	232	88.88	144.4	292	115.55
112.2	234	89.77	145.0	293	116.00
113.3	236	90.66	145.6	294	116.44
114.4	238	91.55	146.7	296	117.33
115.0	239	92.00	147.8	298	118.22
115.6	240	92.44	148.9	300	119.11
116.7	242	93.33	150.0	302	120.00
117.8	244	94.22	151.1	304	120.88
118.9	246	95.11	152.2	306	121.77
120.0	248	96.00	153.3	308	122.66
121.1	250	96.88	154.4	310	123.55
122.2	252	97.77	155.0	311	124.00
123.3	254	98.66	155.6	312	124.44
124.4	256	99.55	156.7	314	125.33
125.0	257	100.00	157.8	316	126.22
125.6	258	100.44	158.9	318	127.11
126.7	260	101.33	160.0	320	128.00
127.8	262	102.22			

DEGREES BAUMÉ AND USES		
Solution	Degrees Baumé	Uses
1 kg sugar + 5 dl water	14–15	granité ices
1 kg sugar + 9 dl water	16–17	water ices, sorbets
1 kg sugar + 112 dl water	20	babas and savarins
1 kg sugar + 115 dl water	28	Pâté à bombe, ice creams
1 kg sugar + 118 dl water	34	crystallisation of fruit
	36	liqueur chocolates
	38	bonbons, coconut ice, marshmallows, fudge

DENSITY

The instrument used for measuring density is the saccharometer, also known as the hydrometer. It is usually made of blown glass, and consists of a bulb, a float and a stem. The bulb carries a quantity of either mercury or small shot at the bottom, adjusted to measure the density of the sugar and water used for the solution.

The principle involved is that any solid body immersed in a liquid displaces its own weight. The stem of the instrument is marked to show how much of the liquid is displaced or, in other words, the density of the liquid. The saccharometer was perfected by the French chemist Antoine Baumé (1728–1804).

Technical processes

Dipping	Fruits, nuts, marzipan
Pouring	Formation of shapes, figures, sweets
Piping	Ornamental displays
Spinning	Classic dishes (croquembouche, St Honoré)
Pulling	Basket weaving, flowers, leaves, ribbons
Blowing	Imitation fruits, figures, swans, peacocks
Rock sugar	Ornamental work

Fondant	Fondant gâteaux, pastries and petits fours
Croquantes	Praline, centrepieces, petits fours
Petits fours	Nougat Montelimar, croquantes, déguisés, mint pastilles, fudge, berlingots, confits (crystallised fruits)

Common faults

1 *Premature crystallisation:* Use of dirty equipment; slow boiling.
2 *Sugar not setting:* Incorrect quantity of glucose or acid; under-cooking.
3 *Sugar sticking to surfaces:* Under-cooked; too much acid.

Points to observe

1 Always use a dry cloth when handling the sugar boiler.
2 Wash the sides of the saucepan down frequently with a brush during boiling, to avoid crystals forming. Always boil the solution very rapidly.
3 Syrups made in advance in large quantities give very good results.
4 Any impurities occurring during boiling should be removed by skimming the surface of the solution.

5   All utensils must be thoroughly cleaned with the aid of an acid, salt and lemon juice, or salt and vinegar, then well rinsed. This should be done just prior to use.

6   Pulling of sugar must be done until it becomes resistant, to attain the desired sheen.

7   Colours are added when the solution has reached the required temperature.

8   Lumps of pulled sugar can be stored in a warm place at a constant temperature, between 50° and 80°C.

9   Cube sugar is always preferred for boiling procedures.

10 Thoroughly dissolve the acid before adding.

11 Always boil to the correct temperature.

12 Use a minimum amount of oil for the working surface.

13 Work on boiled sugar items in a dry atmosphere.

14 Completed items should be stored in hermetically-sealed cabinets. Hygroscopic substances such as quicklime or silicagel can be used to abstract moisture from the air.

15 Always place the boiled sugar saucepan on a saucepan stand.

■ POURED SUGAR *(SUCRE COULÉ)*

Ingredients	
Cube or granulated sugar	1 kg
Water	200 ml
Glucose	60 g

The sugar is boiled to 152–3°C following the basic boiling procedure described on page 14. It is important to observe the rules regarding the cleanliness of all utensils and surfaces used. A good quality marble slab is essential: any cracks or scratches on the surface would make it impossible to remove the poured pieces.

Reduce the heat as the sugar reaches the correct temperature. If any colouring is used, it should be added at about 149–50°C, then continue until the correct temperature is reached. When ready, dip the base of the saucepan in cold water immediately to stop the boiling process.

It is essential to have all the necessary utensils prepared and the surfaces oiled before the sugar reaches the required temperature, as the solution will continue cooking if allowed to stand for any length of time.

Pouring sugar into prepared stencils. Titanium has been added to make the sugar white

An example of poured sugar work. In this case, the sugar has not been coloured

Poured sugar work can take many different forms. Bases are used for the foundation of most centrepieces, either for presentation or for support. The bases are created by pouring the boiled sugar solution into metal moulds, such as flan rings, specially cut rubber moulds, or shapes made from plasticine or rolled marzipan. The rubber or the plasticine should be approximately 4–6 mm thick, depending on the size of the item being produced. Using a clean brush, lightly oil all surfaces and borders coming into contact with the poured solution, to prevent the poured items from sticking to the surface.

Various colours and shapes can be added and artistic creations can be achieved using pre-prepared stencils of the desired shapes. Poured sugar work can take the shape of various figures, such as swans, rabbits, squirrels and cartoon figures, or just poured, then shaped into items such as bowls, basket shapes and candy dishes.

The sugar can be coloured as desired. In this case the colour has to be in liquid form and can be added just prior to the sugar reaching the desired temperature. Items can then be decorated using a paper cornet filled with royal icing.

The poured sugar work can be completed in two ways: The sugar can be left in its natural form, with colour if desired, or calcium carbonate (chalk powder) or titanium dioxide can be added – this will give the solution an opaque appearance, useful for the enhancement of certain figures and shapes, such as the swan, frosted glass windows or the ears, legs and tail of an animal figure.

To obtain the opaque appearance, add 15–20 g of calcium carbonate or titanium dioxide to the basic recipe, diluted in 40 ml of water. Shake it into the boiling sugar as it reaches 145°C and continue boiling to evaporate the added moisture and complete the boiling process.

Boil the sugar to 153°C, then remove from the heat and allow the bubbles to subside. Always pour in a uniform fashion, holding the saucepan close to the marble. Pour slowly and evenly into the prepared shapes, completing the small corners and narrow areas first, then proceeding towards the centre of the shape using a circular motion. Adding more sugar over the completed parts can spoil the effect of the intended design.

Use a spatula to wipe the edge of the saucepan soon after the pouring is complete; do not allow the threads of sugar that extend from the edge of the saucepan to return to the batch.

After the sugar has solidified, carefully remove it from the marble using an oiled palette knife and set it on a cold area of the marble slab. Wipe the edges using a soft tissue, as any oil on the surface will prevent the sugar pieces from sticking together.

Attaching the pieces

The prepared pieces can be welded together using a very small amount of liquid boiled sugar. Alternatively, heat the prepared pieces over a light flame until the surfaces begin to bubble, then immediately stick them together, holding them firmly for a few seconds to obtain a permanent bond.

Storing

The pieces are very fragile. If they are to be stored for use later, extreme care should be taken in packing them. Sugar is very hygroscopic, i.e. it readily absorbs atmospheric moisture. If sugar pieces are exposed to high levels of moisture for extended periods, they will begin to crystallise. Pre-cooked sugar, as well as finished sugar pieces, must be stored in airtight containers with moisture-absorbing agents. Airtight containers can be made of glass or perspex and should be box-shaped, with a false bottom which is then used for moisture-absorbing agents. The relative humidity should be below 10%.

■ MARBLED SUGAR WORK

Follow the recipe and procedures described in the poured sugar section (page 20). Again, it is important to ensure that all utensils and equipment used in the process are clean. The marbled effect can be achieved using three different techniques, although the results will be the same.

Method 1: Partly mix one or more colours in the sugar solution when the boiling stage reaches 153°C. Dip the base of the sugar boiler in cold water to stop the cooking and allow to stand for a few minutes until the bubbles subside. Care is required to ensure that the temperature of the sugar solution does not go above 153°C, as it could be detrimental in obtaining the desired blend of colours.

Method 2: A small amount of colour or colours can be added to the sugar solution just before pouring, swivelling the saucepan to partly blend the colours. The solution can then be poured into the frames or moulds.

Method 3: Marbling effects can be achieved by sprinkling the colours over the surface immediately after the sugar has been poured, using a brush lightly dipped in the colours. The marbled effect can be obtained by spreading the colours with a cocktail stick or the point of a small knife. The process must be completed before the poured sugar sets.

Marbling sugar

Once the poured items are set, they should be removed immediately to a cooler part of the marble slab until required for assembling. It is important to ensure that you have sufficient sugar prepared to complete all

Sugar centrepiece incorporating marbling and piping techniques

he items; if more sugar is required, it would e impossible to obtain identical shades.

Use hot knives to trim or cut edges, if equired. The prepared pieces can be assembled by using more poured sugar or by lightly heating the edges of the pieces until the sugar begins to bubble. A fan will assist in assembling by cooling the sugar.

■ SPUN SUGAR *(SUCRE FILÉ)*

Spun sugar always presents a light, delicate appearance and is used mainly for presentation. It adds an impressive touch to desserts such as:

Ice cream dishes: Coupes, bombes, parfaits, ice cream soufflés, nest shapes for presenting ice creams.

Cold sweets: Mousses, croquembouche, St Honoré, savarins, plated sweets

Gâteaux: Fondant gâteaux, ice cream gâteaux, yule logs.

Centrepieces: Presentation of flowers, filling of sugar baskets, background presentation of figures, petits fours.

Ice-creams presented on a base of spun sugar

Although spun sugar is easy to make, it can sometimes cause considerable trouble. The principle cause of problems in appearance is moisture. During wet weather spun sugar must not be exposed to the atmosphere for long periods: like all sugar work it absorbs moisture, and the innumerable threads of sugar then stick together and cease to glisten.

Spinning sugar

Ingredients

Cube or granulated sugar	500 g
Water	100 ml
Glucose	40 g

Equipment

Saucepan
Stand for saucepan
Spinning whisk
Wooden handles

Prepare and cook the sugar solution as described on page 14. As soon as the sugar solution has reached the required temperature (150°C) remove the saucepan from the heat and dip the base in cold water for a couple of minutes to stop the boiling. Place the pan on a triangle and allow to stand longer for the solution to thicken, occasionally swivelling the saucepan to even out the texture of the solution.

Prepare all the necessary utensils well in advance and cover the floor with paper or trays to prevent it becoming sticky with sugar. Lay two or three broom handles on a table or work surface so that they hang over the edge. Holding the sugar boiler in one hand, dip the whisk in the boiled sugar with the other, then raise the whisk and shake it backwards and forwards. The sugar will fall over the handles in long threads. Continue until there is enough spun sugar. Wait a few minutes for the sugar to cool, then place two hands under the sugar and lift it onto a clean surface. Roll up very

lightly. Use immediately, if possible, or store ready-shaped in hermetically-sealed deep trays to prevent the sugar absorbing moisture.

To use for decoration, keep the spun sugar as light as possible, place on the dish at the latest stage possible, and do not completely mask the subject to be decorated.

If all the spun sugar is not used in the one operation, it can be kept in a dry, clean place and re-heated when needed. Re-heat in the oven with the door left open, then re-spin as required. This shows that it is not always necessary to boil sugar afresh each time spun sugar is needed. In first-class hotels and restaurants it is often required at various times during the day, as the orders arrive.

■ ROCK SUGAR *(SUCRE ROCHER)*

Rock sugar is mostly used for decorating purposes: the name derives from its porous, rock-like appearance. The sugar can be coloured as desired. It can also be pushed through a coarse sieve and the powder used for decorating gâteaux and pastries.

Ingredients

Cube or granulated sugar	500 g
Water	200 ml
Royal icing	30 g
(No lemon juice)	

Equipment

Saucepan
Spatula
Sieve
Bowl for icing
Saucepan lid
Saucepan stand
Foil
Metal tray

Prepare and boil the sugar as described in the basic sugar boiling method, making sure that all utensils are clean and free from grease. It is essential to have the working surface oiled and the utensils at hand before putting on the sugar to boil.

Line a stainless steel saucepan with foil and add the sugar and water. The pan should be large enough so that it is not more than one-third full.

Boil the solution to 138°C, washing down the sides of the saucepan occasionally using a brush – this helps to cook the sugar uniformly. When the required temperature is reached, immediately remove the pan from the heat and quickly stir in the prepared royal icing (page 54) using a wooden spatula. As soon as the royal icing is blended in, cover the pan with a tight-fitting lid and return to a low heat until the sugar rises to the top of the pan. This will only take a few minutes – if left too long, it will spoil the desired whiteness. To remove the mass of sugar from the saucepan, loosen the foil from the sides of the saucepan as soon as it is removed from the heat and turn out onto a metal tray.

When the royal icing is added to the syrup there is considerable frothing: the saucepan lid should be fitted on as quickly as possible.

Alternative technique: Realistic rock effects can be achieved simply by placing a small amount of pastillage (in a suitable dish or bowl) in the microwave oven. Cook for approximately 4 to 5 minutes, depending on the amount used. The result will be very realistic with a perfectly white colour and volcanic texture, ideal for decorating Christmas cakes or modelling.

■ FONDANT

Fondant is the base for most soft, creamy-textured sweets, gâteaux and pastries. All confectioners are familiar with the techniques involved in using it, though it is generally bought ready-made: it hardly pays to make it yourself, because of the time involved and the difficulty of achieving a uniform texture and colour.

Ingredients

Cube or granulated sugar	1 kg
Water	120 ml
Glucose	50 g

Equipment

Sugar boiler
Thermometer
4 iron bars
Metal scraper
Palette knife
Damp cloth
Storage container with lid

Prepare all the utensils and sprinkle the marble surface with water. Arrange the metal bars to form a square, keeping the corners well sealed: this is to prevent the solution running over the edge of the slab.

Boil the sugar as described on page 14.

Add the glucose as soon as the solution comes to the boil and immerse the sugar thermometer, removing any scum on the surface. Boil rapidly until the temperature reaches 118°C. Pour the sugar onto the marble surface and sprinkle cold water over the top to prevent a skin forming. Allow to stand for a few minutes.

With a metal scraper in one hand and a palette knife in the other, turn the fondant over and over until it becomes white and thick, with a creamy texture. Cover the fondant with a damp cloth and leave until cold. Store in an airtight container and use as required.

1 Fondant should not be worked the moment it is poured on the slab or it may 'grain', i.e. become sugary.
2 A few drops of blue food colouring will help to preserve the whiteness of the fondant.

Using fondant

To use fondant, place the required amount in a saucepan (for dipping purposes a sauteuse is an advantage, as the top is large and not too deep). Add a small amount of stock syrup – the amount varies according to the thickness of the fondant – then, using a wooden spatula, stir the fondant over a low heat until it becomes smooth, creamy in texture and free from lumps. The temperature of the fondant, particularly for dipping or covering gâteaux, is very important and should not exceed 37°C (blood heat). If the fondant is over-heated the gloss will disappear and the items produced will become dull in appearance.

The consistency of the fondant depends on what it is being used for: eclairs require a thicker consistency, but for coating sponges or gâteaux it would have to be thinner. If chocolate couverture is used, this will thicken the fondant – extra stock syrup should therefore be added.

Where fondant is used to coat sponges (an absorbent surface) they should always be coated first with a thin layer of marzipan or boiled apricot jam.

Fondant can be coloured or flavoured, remembering that the colour should always be a pastel shade. Liqueurs can also be added as required, but this may alter the texture of the fondant; the amount of stock syrup should be reduced and replaced with the liqueur.

The left-over fondant is simply scraped back into the saucepan and the sides of the saucepan cleaned down. Pour cold water over the top to prevent a skin forming. Keep for further use, pouring away the water and re-warming the fondant when required.

ITALIAN MERINGUE (MERINGUE ITALIENNE)

Ingredients	
Egg whites	$\frac{1}{2}$ litre
Cube sugar	400 g–1.5 kg
Water to saturation	

The soft, creamy texture of Italian meringue will provide excellent aeration in mousses, creams, cold and iced cream soufflés, and also acts as an excellent stabiliser for sorbets. It is ideal for producing omelettes surprises and helps in piping decoration.

Make sure that all utensils used are perfectly clean and completely free from any traces of grease, as this will break down the structure of the egg whites and prevent it reaching the desired volume. It is also essential to avoid any traces of egg yolk in with the whites.

Italian meringue can be coloured and flavoured by adding compounds when near completion. As in 'cold meringue' or 'swiss meringue', use double the weight of sugar to egg white to produce a lighter texture; the amount of sugar can start from 400 g per litre of egg whites. Boil the saturated solution, following the techniques and precautions described in sugar boiling (page 14), until the required temperature is reached:

118°C Soft ball: mousses, cold and iced soufflés
221°C Hard ball: *Soufflés surprises*
138°C Small crack: Nougat Montelimar

While the boiling sugar reaches the required temperature, use a scalded mixing bowl and whisk the egg white until a firm snowy texture is obtained. Very slowly but continuously, pour in the boiled sugar in a steady stream while whisking. Continue until the meringue has attained the required texture, then continue whisking at a lower speed until the meringue is cold.

Points to observe

1 Only use stainless steel or copper bowls.
2 Ensure all utensils are free from grease.
3 Ensure the egg whites are free from grease.
4 Avoid leaving traces of egg yolk in the whites.
5 The egg whites should reach the snowy texture at the same time as the boiled sugar reaches the correct temperature.
6 Use the meringue as soon as produced, but it can be stored in a sealed container when completely cold.
7 Do not over-whip the whites, as they will break up and lose volume.
8 If the sugar is added to the meringue before the snowy texture is reached, the meringue will collapse, lose volume and become runny.

9 Continue whisking until the meringue is cold.

■ PIPING SUGAR

Use your imagination to pipe a wide range of masterpieces, entirely made from boiled sugar. This is a recently developed art, practised by professional pâtissiers for simple and quickly produced centrepieces. To produce effective items requires constant practice to attain the necessary skills.

Equipment
Sugar boiler
Marble slab
Alcohol burner
Paper cornets
Thick cloth or oven gloves

Follow the basic sugar boiling procedure (page 14), omitting the tartaric acid and cooking the sugar to 145–8°C. Place the base of the sugar boiler into cold water for a couple of minutes to stop the boiling. Allow the sugar to stand for about 5–8 minutes to attain a thicker consistency; this is important to ensure that the sugar will not run from the cornet too fast while piping.

Clean and lightly oil the marble slab, and produce a number of double-layer paper cornets. Half-fill the cornet with the sugar, fold in the corners of the cornet and roll to seal in the sugar tightly. Cut the cornet, using scissors, to the thickness required for the item being produced (the larger the item, the thicker the thread). Lifting the cornet 5–8 cm from the surface, allow the sugar to flow over the prepared pattern. Avoid stopping while the piping is in progress as this will harden the sugar at the tip of the cornet and make it difficult to re-start piping.

Make a paper cornet for piping

If the cornet gets accidentally clogged with hard sugar, it is easier to re-start the piping using a fresh cornet.

As soon as the piped item is cold, it can be loosened from the surface by pushing gently from the base. Place all the prepared items on a fresh area of the lightly oiled marble slab, or on silicone paper, until ready to assemble.

Attach the pieces together by using more piped sugar or by gently heating the edges over the burner. Cold air from the fan will help to harden the melted sugar in position.

Piping a sugar fountain

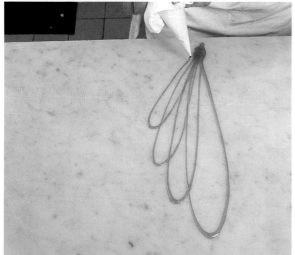

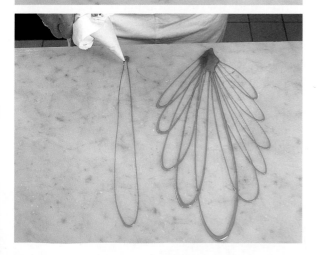

■ PULLING SUGAR

Pulled sugar work is a very delicate art, demanding a great deal of practice and, more particularly, observation. Before starting to explain the techniques involved, it is important to mention a few of the pitfalls, caused by wrong ingredients, or incorrect boiling or handling of sugar.

1　If insufficient glucose is added to the solution, which is then boiled to the required temperature, you will find after it is pulled and ready for shaping that it breaks and is hard to work.

2　If too much glucose is added to the solution, which is then boiled to the required temperature, it will be quite easy to work after it is pulled and ready for shaping. Shortly afterwards, however, the sugar will become greasy and shiny, with a sticky smear like thick syrup.

3　If the solution is allowed to boil above the required temperature, until it is nearly brown, it will be greasy and sticky when pulled. It should not then be used for any ornamental work, but could be used for bases in the form of croquant, or turned into caramel.

4　If the sugar is undercooked and then poured on the marble slab for pulling, it will stick to everything it touches – the palette knife, the slab and the hands – making it impossible to achieve satisfactory results. Continuing to pull would result in a grainy texture. All you can do with the sugar in that condition is to re-heat, add more water, and boil to obtain a syrup.

5　Do not boil large quantities, or more than can possibly be pulled in one session; 1–1½ kg is enough to pull successfully.

Ingredients

Cube or granulated sugar	500 g
Water	100 ml
Glucose or tartaric acid	60 g
Lemon juice	15 ml
Vegetable oil or liquid-paraffin for the marble slab	
Colours as required	

Equipment

Sugar boiler
Scissors
Metal scraper
Saucepan stand
Palette knife
Thermometer
Strainer for the scum
Container for lemon juice
Container for oil
Heating system
Infra-red lamp

Instructions concerning the hygiene of all utensils and working surfaces being used must be strictly followed. Before beginning the sugar boiling, the operator has to get accustomed to handling the bulk sugar at a high temperature; this can be easily achieved after some practice. Avoid working with oily hands, and always use thick dry cloths when handling the hot sugar boiler.

Ensure all utensils are at hand by the working surface, and rub the marble slab with vegetable oil or liquid-paraffin, using a tissue. Switch on the infra-red lamp to keep the sugar soft and to store it once pulled.

Make the sugar solution and heat gently to boiling point. Add the glucose or tartaric acid and boil rapidly until the sugar has reached 153°C, washing down the sides of the saucepan with a pastry brush as necessary.

The sugar at this stage should have an amber colour, which shows it has reached the correct temperature. Remove from the heat and dip the base of the saucepan in iced water for a few moments, then place on a saucepan stand. Shake in the lemon juice and colour, then pour onto the prepared area of the marble slab. Fill the saucepan with water and put on to boil, to wash out the remaining sugar.

Allow the poured sugar to settle on the marble for a few minutes to form a skin underneath, then, using a palette knife, turn the edges in towards the centre; repeat this process about three times until you can slide the palette knife under the sugar, lift it up and drop it back on the surface.

Turn it over and repeat the procedure until it is possible to start pulling by holding the sugar with one hand and stretching it out with the other. Bring both ends together then repeat the operation 15–18 times until the whole mass becomes firmer but still pliable. The resulting mass should have a bright sheen, which is always pronounced on pulled sugar items.

Fold in the edges

Pulling sugar

Pour the boiled sugar onto a marble slab

Turn it over and repeat the process until it is possible to start pulling the sugar

Pull by hand

As soon as the sugar is sufficiently pulled, cut it into two or three pieces. Roll each piece into a ball and place in a warm place, on the heating system and under the infra-red lamp, to maintain its smooth soft texture. There are various ways of storing the pulled sugar: I prefer to use small non-stick tin containers.

It is important to understand what actually happens to the small bulk of sugar while being pulled. Air is being introduced into the mass while the hot sugar is twisted manually. Molecules of air and sugar combined form a framework similar to the structure of a beehive. This configuration is the basis that allows it to be pulled into various shapes, and to be blown to the structure required.

Infra-red heating system for keeping pulled sugar at a constant temperature

■ SHAPING PULLED SUGAR

Sugar pulling is a delicate art that demands great versatility – but the techniques can be acquired through much practice. In this technique the satin-like fragility of pulled sugar is combined with its ability to stretch when heated. Because the surface temperature is cooler than the internal temperature, as the sugar is pulled the surface acquires hundreds of microscopic cracks and ridges – it is the light reflecting off this surface that gives the illusion of a satin-like finish. This illusion can best be achieved when the mass of sugar is aerated to capacity and pulled to its maximum length. It is when the surface is exposed to excessive moisture, from the infra-red bulb or oven heat, that the ridges dissolve and the sugar loses its satiny appearance. It is important to keep the sugar under the infra-red lamp and occasionally turn it over to maintain an even distribution of temperature. During the pulling process, always pull the sugar by the edges – excessive handling will quickly cool the sugar and necessitate re-heating. It is also important to maintain a uniform thickness – stretching gently and continuously, rather than giving sharp pulls.

Place the pulled completed items on silicone paper in a safe, dry place, and store at room temperature. If the items are to be stored for longer periods, then it may be necessary to keep them in a hermetically-sealed tray with some absorbing agents.

Enhancing the appearance of pulled leaves and flowers very often depends on the colourings. Too much colour blended in the boiled sugar can interfere with the texture, and sometimes this spoils the desired silky look. The quality of the colour used is therefore essential. I recommend using only liquid colours, as paste colours may cause the sugar to grain. One of the best, and oldest, methods of colouring boiled sugar is to add powder colours dissolved in alcohol; the liquid evaporates when added to the boiled sugar. Use the minimum amount necessary. The colour can be improved by brushing colour or dusting powders on the finished item: a range of lustre colours is available.

Leaves

Making and wiring pulled sugar leaves

Pull the required amount of sugar

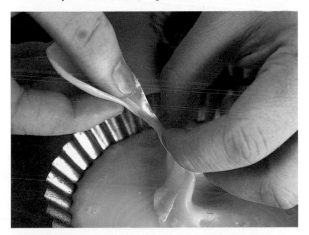

Nip off the end

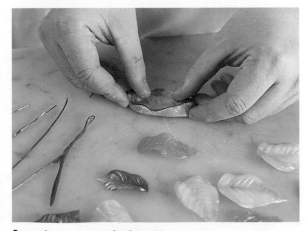

Press the sugar on a leaf mould

Coat a wire with sugar

Attach leaves to the wire

Prepare the pulled sugar as previously descri-bed, making sure it is the right colour. Remember that, to produce realistic leaves, the colour has to be luminous and there may be more than one shade on each leaf.

Using the thumb and forefinger, pinch and pull the required amount of sugar (keep-ing the stored sugar under the lamp) to a thin, nearly transparent round shape; then break it off with the other hand, ensuring that you form a pointed end. Immediately press the sugar on a leaf mould to attain the vein pattern. If the mould is not available, place the leaf on a warm surface and quickly mark the veins using a knife, or lay the leaf on a large clean potato and mark with a knife.

Hold the leaf under the lamp for about 6 seconds, or until the sugar is pliable, and then gently twist it to simulate the natural bend of a leaf. Any modification, like serrating the edges, must be done under the lamp. Place the completed leaf in the storage container for later use.

Rose leaves: Round and pointed, the edges serrated using scissors.

Apple leaves: Round and pointed, very lightly serrated; use a hot knife.

Pear leaves: Slightly longer than the apple, with similar finish.

Strawberry leaves: Round, serrated, similar to the apple leaves but smaller.

Ivy and grape leaves: Prepare a round shape out of the sugar, then cut with scissors, using a stencil as guidance (the stencil can be prepared by cutting a piece of firm plastic to the required shape of the leaf). Ivy leaves can also be made by assembling three overlapping rose leaves, sticking them together while soft.

Daffodil leaves: Long and narrow, gradually ending in a point with the top end curled over.

Tulip leaves: Similar to the daffodil, but larger at the base and left straight.

WIRING THE LEAVES
Prepare the wires – cut to the correct length and coat with sugar. As soon as the leaf is made, heat the tip end of the wire and press it into the leaf; hold for a few seconds for the sugar to set. Colour and shade as desired.

Flowers

Pull the sugar as described, using the appro-priate colour. It is important to pull the sugar until it has a bright sheen. Roll the sugar into a ball and place under the heating system for storage. Pre-heated sugar, such as that left over from a previous session, can be used again by gradually warming the bulk at low heat. Give it a quick pull to bring back the sheen, and the sugar is again ready for shaping.

Once the art of shaping flowers from pulled sugar is mastered, very little knowl-edge is required to fix these in shape. Where possible a real flower should be used as a guide, especially when making flowers with several colours, such as orchids.

Note: Never attempt any finishing proce-dure (bending, spreading, twisting or curling) on the petals unless the sugar is pliable. Thin pulled sugar petals are extremely fragile and will cool quickly and become rigid after they have been made. To prevent them breaking, always heat them under the infra-red bulb until they are pliable before handling them.

ROSES
Start by making the centre of the flower, the bud. Using the thumb and forefinger, stretch and shape a small strip of pulled sugar over

Making a pulled sugar rose

Pull a small amount of sugar over the thumb to create a rose petal

Add a second petal to the bud

Nip off the end

Attach the other petals

Shape the petal into a bud

Add the calyx

the thumb to create a very thin semicircle. If not sufficiently thin, it can be stretched further. Detach by breaking off the sugar remaining at the end of the thumb. As you move your fingers away from under the lamp, the sugar will immediately harden and come away from the thumb – the shape of your thumb will have given the thin layer of sugar a natural petal shape.

Curl over the first petal in the shape of a thin hollow cylinder: this will serve as the bud for the centre of the rose. (If the rose has to have a wire support, produce a cone shape and insert a hooked wire in the broad base.)

Produce the first petal in the same way as the bud, slightly curling the top edges over while the sugar is still hot, and maintaining the concave shape formed by the thumb. Attach it to the centre bud, heating the base over the oil lamp flame. Repeat the process for the second and third petals, attaching them round the centre, matching the height of the centre with the petals and slightly curling the petals back as they are attached. The rose can

also be assembled by overlapping the petals as they are attached, giving the centre of the rose a spiral effect. With three petals this could be used as a small bud rose, adding the calyx to complete the flower.

For larger flowers, make the third petal slightly bigger and attach this, the fourth and fifth petals round the centre, as described. Now make another five petals, again slightly larger. As the petals are produced, place them on a piece of fabric, away from the heat. These last petals can be attached to the base of the rose by holding the rose upside down and slightly heating the base of the petals over a flame. This way, the last petals will hang slightly.

If the rose is to be wired, form a small ball of sugar and attach it to the sugar-coated wire (determine the length of the stem by measuring the sugar basket or vase before coating the wire with the sugar). Shape this ball into a cone shape and allow it to get cold. Using a heated, pointed knife, make a small hole at the base of the rose, then heat the wired cone over a small flame and place it in the hole, holding it for a few seconds to set.

It is also possible to fit the calyx at the base of the rose. This can be done by pulling a petal shape of green sugar. Attach it at the base of the rose with the pointed end pointing up and curved outwards; four or five leaves per rose are necessary. Always store the completed flowers away from the heat in sealed containers, protected from moisture.

To assemble leaves for roses, produce five wired leaves as previously described (page 36) using 28 gauge florist's wire. Twist the wires tightly, keeping one leaf ahead at the top end, with the other four following – giving the stem of leaves a realistic appearance.

CARNATIONS
The petals of carnations are pulled in the same way as those of roses, but cut into thin triangu-

lar shapes. The ends of the triangles are then chiselled or chipped with scissors. When all the petals have been prepared, store away from the heat. This preparation has to be done quickly – the whole process must be done without removing your hands from under the lamp, as the sugar will harden very quickly.

The next operation is to give the chiselled portion an S shape. Three of the smallest petals can then be heated over a flame and pressed one into the other to form the centre. Four other larger petals are stuck round these, the petals fitting one into the other, and then surrounded by eight still larger petals.

If a stem is required, use the same technique as the rose. The underside of the carnation can then be completed by adding a number of very small arrow-shaped leaves to represent the calyx. The leaves of the carnation are long and narrow and can be attached directly to the stem. A bouquet of light-coloured carnations can be formed by placing darker coloured flowers in the centre, including the speckled variety. The speckled effect is obtained by flicking a brush dipped in colour over the flower.

DAFFODILS

Prepare the pulled sugar as described, adding yellow colouring to the boiled sugar before pouring. Store under the lamp to keep warm. Pull six petals per flower. Each should be about 5–6 cm long and 2.5 cm wide, with a pointed end. As each petal is made press it to a completed one, forming a circular fan shape with the points facing outwards. Each petal has to be curved outwards: this can be achieved by warming the shape under the lamp.

To form a trumpet shape for the centre of the flower, pull a small amount of sugar into a small strip, about 2.5–3 cm wide and 4–5 cm in length. Holding the strip under the lamp, crimp all along one side with scissors, then roll it round your finger to form a bell shape and

press to join the edges. Curve the crimped edges outwards. Immediately, touch the base of the bell to the flame and attach it to the centre of the fan.

Pull out a small thread of yellow sugar and cut, using scissors, into five or six 4 cm lengths. Using tweezers, gently heat one end of each length and quickly dip in yellow-coloured caster sugar. Allow to set. Again using tweezers, heat the other end of each length and attach to the centre of the trumpet to form the stamens.

ORCHIDS

Prepare the pulled sugar as described. You can use your imagination over the many shapes and colours of orchids, though the colours should always be pastel. The centres can be tinted with deeper colours when the flowers are complete. Form three leaf-shaped strips of pulled sugar and attach the ends together, then produce two petal shapes, similar to the rose petals. Undulate the top end of the petals by warming the ends under the lamp, maintaining a concave shape. Fix the two petals in the centre of the other three.

For the centre prepare another petal shape, a larger folded cone shape, and fix this petal in the centre with the tip end folded backwards. Complete the centre of the flower with a thin spadix dipped in coloured caster sugar, inserted down the throat of the cone. Colour the inside of the flowers with darker shades using coloured dusting powders. The inside of the cone can be dotted with a deeper colour, using a cocktail stick. The orchid can be fitted to the end of a sugar-coated wire, gauge 22.

Baskets

A woven basket offers many possibilities for presentation: for cold buffets, sweet trolleys, competitions or exhibitions. It can be used to

Making a pulled sugar basket

Hold the pulled sugar in a pear shape and weave
it in and out of the frame

Let one row drop naturally over the other

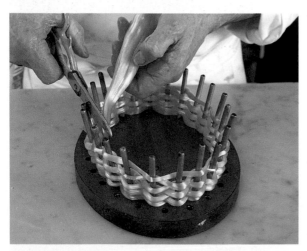

Clip the sugar when finished – leave the end
inside the frame so it doesn't show

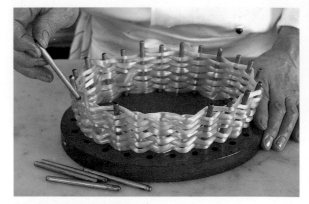

Remove the metal rods

Insert sugar rods

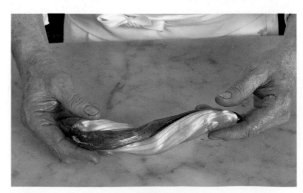

Twist two colours together to form a rope

Put sugar ropes on the top and bottom of the basket

serve petits fours, chocolates, sugar flowers and blown sugar fruits. The basket is woven just as a straw basket would be, but in this case the material is a shimmering strand of pulled sugar.

Follow the recipe and procedure described in the pulling sugar section (page 32). It is very important to use the correct amount of lemon juice, to give the sugar an adequate pull, and to place it in the storage containers under the infra-red lamp.

Wind sugar around a strong wire to form the handle

Equipment
Infra-red lamp
Heating system
Sugar boiler
Containers for water, oil, colours, lemon juice
Marble slab
Palette knife
Knife
Scissors
Basket frame
Wire for the handle
Cake board
Hair drier
Alcohol burner
Metal scraper

The basket frame can be made in any shape – round, oval or square – and any size. The average size is about 20–24 cm. The base is normally made of wood, with an *uneven* number of holes round the edge (about 19, 21 or 23, set 2–3 cm apart) to hold the rods. These should be 10–15 cm in length, and made of wood or metal. It is important to ensure that the rods are set at an angle. The fit should be accurate, but you must be able to remove the rods easily when the sugar weaving is complete.

Set the rods in position and oil very lightly, including the base.

Cook sufficient sugar to make a complete basket out of one batch, to ensure a uniform colour; it would be difficult to obtain the same shade from a second batch of sugar. 500 g of sugar should be sufficient to produce a single basket, and 750 g of sugar for a double basket, including the handle.

To give the basket a realistic colour, use the sugar in its natural form, cooking it to a light golden colour: this will give the pulled sugar a straw look. Use the sugar as soon as it is pulled, or give the pliable sugar from under the lamp a couple of pulls to brighten and unify the texture. Only use part of the batch of sugar at one time; if it then goes hard, it can be exchanged for a softer one. Hold the pulled sugar in a pear shape; this will prevent the sugar from cooling too quickly. Pull out a pencil-thick strand, and start weaving round the frame, in and out of the rods.

As you return to the starting position continue the second round, allowing it to drop over the first one: there should be no need to push the strand down, and it will have a much better appearance if it settles in place naturally. Continue weaving until the top of the frame is reached. Do not weave the sugar tight to the top of the basket – leave about 5 mm of space to enable you to remove the rods. If the strand breaks accidentally, try to finish with

the end inside the frame; the weaving can then be re-started by attaching the strand where it left off.

If a double basket is required, gently remove the rods when the basket is completed, carefully wiggling them out of the base. Carefully turn the frame upside down, and store away from heat until required. Fit the rods back in the frame and start again, producing another basket just like the first. Make sure the basket is robust and stable; the structure can be reinforced if necessary by sticking strips of soft pulled sugar inside the basket, where they will not be seen from the outside. Remove the rods as before.

The metal rods can now be replaced with sugar ones. These are produced by pulling out a long pencil-shaped strand, until the required size is reached. Lay it on the work surface and use a heated knife to cut the sugar into rods the same height as the basket. Insert the rods in the appropriate places to complete both baskets.

The next step is to produce the coiled rope that sits at the top and bottom of the woven edge. Pull out two long strands of the same pulled sugar and twist them together to form a rope-like shape. Place the coil at the base of the basket, cutting off the surplus with scissors or a heated knife. Repeat the process for the top of the basket.

Complete the double basket by welding the second basket on top of the first upside-down basket. The join can be finished neatly with another rope, or by placing a narrow ribbon to cover the join; add a bow if desired.

If a handle is required, this can be produced by coiling a strong wire, cut and curved to the correct shape; the wire should reach the base of the basket and fit inside. Again, using a lump of pulled sugar in the shape of a pear, pull out a pencil-shaped strand and start winding it round the wire, starting from the middle of the handle. Wind evenly and continuously until the end of the wire is reached. Repeat the process for the other side.

Place the prepared handle inside the basket, using strips of soft pulled sugar to ensure that the handle is fixed firmly, since it may eventually support ribbon, flowers, etc., if required.

A sugar ribbon can be wrapped round the handle as soon as it is produced (see page 44). Allow the ribbon to drape down the sides and over the base of the basket. The inside of the basket can be filled with a blown polythene bag, or a lump of pulled sugar can be blown inside the basket to make it look full. Petits fours or blown fruits can then sit on top for display.

Double basket with blown fruits

Ribbons

Making pulled sugar ribbons is a very delicate procedure but, with practice, satisfactory results can be obtained.

Pulling sugar for ribbons will never produce the same result twice, so it is essential that sufficient coloured sugar is produced and pulled to complete the project. The elegant satin-like shine and fragility of pulled sugar can be displayed to full effect in a centrepiece of ribbons, flowers and blown sugar items, demonstrating the remarkable range of sugar work possible.

Equipment

Sugar boiler
Palette knife
Scraper
Large knife
Thermometer
Marble slab
Infra-red lamp
Heating system
Scissors
Large tray
Silicone paper
Hair drier

Pulling a sugar ribbon

Fasten together different-coloured strips of sugar

Stretch to approximately four times its length and cut in half

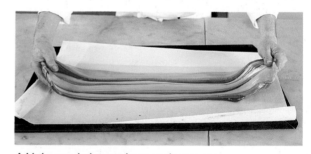

Add the two halves and repeat the process

A two-colour striped ribbon is created by fastening together five narrow rectangular strips of sugar, about 1 cm wide and 3 cm thick. Use three of one colour (ideally a darker shade) and two of another. Fasten the strips close together while the sugar is warm, soft and pliable. Alternate the shades, with the darker shade on the outside.

The overall size of the rectangle should be approximately 12–15 cm long, 7–8 cm wide and 3 cm thick. Pinch one end of the striped rectangle and pull evenly into a thin band.

Two basic techniques are used for producing a pulled sugar ribbon; the first one is

Stretch the sugar (method 2) – massage the sugar while pulling

Stretch until the correct thickness is attained

Shape the sugar as required

most suitable for the beginner. It is essential to keep the sugar, under the infra-red lamp, in a uniform malleable texture.

Method 1: Place a baking tray, lined with silicone paper, under the lamp. Hold the strip at each end and pull evenly, stretching it to approximately four times its original length. Lay the strip on the prepared warm tray, cut in half and immediately place the two pieces side by side, ensuring that both lengths are stuck well together. Pull the strip again to stretch and reduce the thickness (again to about four times its length). This procedure can be repeated twice more. Rubbing the whole length of the ribbon over the knee, covered with an apron, assists in producing an even thickness of ribbon. Continue stretching until the desired width is achieved.

Pulling the ribbon steadily will help to prevent the sugar cracking and setting before the correct thickness is achieved. Using scissors or a heated knife, cut the ribbon to the approximate length required. If used for a basket, the ribbon has to be wrapped over the handle as quickly as possible, then trimmed to size using a warm knife. A hair drier, blowing warm or cold air, will help in curving and shaping the ribbon.

Method 2: For the second technique, two people are needed to achieve satisfactory results. Prepare the pulled coloured sugar rectangle and pull the ribbon as described in Method 1. At the last stage, one person can then hold one end of the strip, while the other starts to stretch the ribbon evenly and gradually. If you simultaneously rub the ribbon with the palm of the hands, this will help to even out the thickness. As soon as the required length and width is achieved, place the ribbon on a cold surface, oiled or lined with silicone paper, and cut to the size required using a warm knife.

These operations must be executed rapidly while the sugar is hot. With practice, it is possible to pull a very thin, even-sized ribbon. Start by making short pieces, which are easier to do and require no assistance.

MAKING BOWS

Lay the completed ribbon on the work surface and, using a warm knife, cut pieces approximately 12–15 cm in length. Hold each piece under the lamp for a few moments until it begins to soften, then remove from the heat and bend over in half so the ends touch, making a loop. Gently heat the ends over a flame, then squeeze to form a pleated end: this will give the bow a realistic appearance.

Use 10–12 loops to make an attractive bow; 4–5 should be adequate to decorate a sugar basket. Heat the ends of two loops together and allow to set. Continue with the other loops and arrange in a circular fashion, followed with a comet tail if desired.

Making a sugar bow

Cut pieces approximately 12–15 cm in length and make loops

Assemble the bow

■ BLOWING PULLED SUGAR
(SUCRE SOUFFLÉ)

Perfection in blown sugar can only be achieved with dedication, practice and a great deal of patience. Although many different blown sugar shapes can be made, as well as centrepieces, there are two basic shapes:

The sphere: Large, such as lemon, apple, peach, lemon, pear, orange, etc; small, such as strawberry, cherry, grape, etc.

The altered sphere: Banana, dolphin, swan, peacock, bottle, vase, and various animal figures.

The sphere is created by blowing a solid lump of pulled sugar into a round ball. The altered sphere is created by making a hollow cylindrical shape.

Follow the ingredients and procedure described in the sugar pulling section (page 32). Again, the cleanliness of all surfaces and utensils is paramount.

Equipment

Marble slab
Sugar boiler
Palette knife
Large knife
Metal scraper
Thermometer
Container for lemon juice and oil
Scraper
Scissors
Heating system
Blowing tubes, or hand and foot blowing pump
Fan
Alcohol burner

It is important to acquire the correct-sized blowing tubes: 10 mm tubes for larger items and smaller tubes (3, 5, 8 mm) for smaller items. Blowing pumps are essential for most items. The foot pump leaves the hands free to manipulate the item being blown. The hand pump, which has an ingeniously designed

Equipment for blowing sugar

valve so that no air can return while blowing, gives the best results; it also stops any criticisms related to blowing over food, as the equipment complies with food hygiene regulations.

Basic procedure

Make sure the sugar is malleable before attempting to use it for blowing, and always begin blowing under the lamp, moving in front of a fan to complete the item. Select the appropriate blowing tube, then cut off a lump of sugar with scissors; the size will depend on the size of the item to be produced.

1　Form the sugar into a smooth ball (cylinder shape for the altered spheres).
2　Push a finger into the ball of sugar to make a pocket. For small items (cherry) use the end of a pen.
3　Warm the end of the tube.
4　Attach the end of the tube to the mouth of the pocket, to produce a chamber of air. Completely seal the sugar to the tube.
5　Start to blow gently and steadily, rotating the tube.
6　As the air chamber begins to expand, gradually shape the item, using your hands to make the necessary adjustments.
7　Introduce cold air from the fan as soon as the sugar begins to take shape.
8　Cool completely, using the fan.
9　Using a warm knife, cut off the surplus sugar.
10　Place the blown item away from the heat and complete as required.

MOUTH BLOWING PROCESS
Make sure the sugar is tightly sealed round the blowing tube, so that the air being blown in is kept inside the sugar sphere.

Hold the pipe slightly above the horizontal and blow evenly, slowly rotating the pipe. It is essential to blow softly as the air begins to expand. Do not allow the sugar to twist at the end of the tube during rotation. Cup your hand round the expanding ball to control the pressure, which has to be increased gradually and uniformily. Continue the process about 25–30 cm from the infra-red lamp, depending on the size of the item being blown. Continue blowing until the ball is completely full of air and has an even thickness. As the shape begins to appear, move from the lamp and face the fan to complete the blowing, rotating the tube continually. Any additional shaping must be done at this stage, though the item can be put back under the lamp for a few moments if necessary in order to produce shapes such as peach, apple, pear, etc.

Making a blown sugar peach

Begin blowing

Make a hollow in the sugar with your finger

Expand the sphere under the hot lamp

Insert the blowing tube and close the sugar tightly round it

Continue shaping in front of the fan to cool the sugar

Cut with a hot knife

Gently make the indentations in the peach

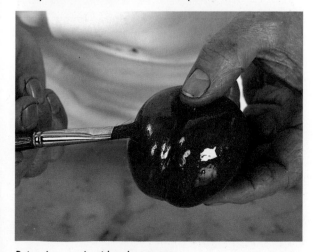

Paint the peach with colour paste

Keep the blown sugar item under the fan until completely cold. Avoid pressing it with the hands, as you can damage or mark the surface.

A foot pump can also be used to blow sugar

Blowing fruits

APPLES

Follow the instructions for the mouth blowing process (page 47). Again, the sugar should be malleable and not too soft. Cut off a lump of sugar from the batch under the lamp, using scissors. Untinted sugar could be used, as the colours can be brushed on when the shape is completed or a small amount of green can be added when the sugar has reached the correct temperature (153°C). Attach the sugar to the blowing tube, seal to prevent the air from escaping, and blow softly and evenly while rotating the blowing tube until the air has filled the ball. Carefully pull the sugar away from the end of the blowing tube to create a margin. Continue to blow, facing the fan to begin the cooling of the sugar, until the sphere reaches approximately 5–6 cm in diameter.

Blown sugar fruits

When nearly cold, make a 5–6 cm indentation at each end of the sphere to resemble an apple. When completely cold, cut the sugar away from the tube with a warm knife. Using your fingernails, pinch the soft sugar where it has just been cut and pull out a strand to form the stem. Leave the apple in front of the fan to cool as fast as possible. The stem could also be attached separately, using a tiny bit of sugar. Store away from heat.

Hold the fruit in your hands. Using a sable brush, gently brush the surface with deep red colour. Use a striking flip effect to produce streaks of red in parts of the fruit to simulate the apple. The stem can be coloured brown.

STRAWBERRIES

The size and shape of strawberries varies a great deal. The best size to make is 40 mm long and 30–35 mm wide at the top, tapering to a rounded point at the bottom. A 30 mm ball of red-coloured pulled sugar should be sufficient. Attach it to a 6–7 mm gauge blowing tube and, working under the infra-red lamp, blow softly, rotating the tube and sugar until partly filled with air. Using the tips of the fingers, pull out the top half of the sphere to a rounded point. Gently pull the sugar away from the tube to create a margin, maintaining a tapered shape. As the strawberry forms into shape, cool it in front of the fan until completely cold. Use a warm knife to cut the sugar at the base and to flatten the end. Cool quickly. Using dark green pulled sugar, pull out five little leaf shapes, slightly curved, and let them set away from the heat. Heat the base of the leaves over a flame and attach to the flattened base of the strawberry. Attach a small stem. To simulate the strawberry seeds, carefully heat the point of a small knife over a flame and make tiny indentations all over the surface. Complete by brushing red colour all over the surface of the fruit, and touch up the stem using dark green colour. If the fruit is to be suspended, use wired stems in the fruit.

CHERRIES

Use deep-red pulled sugar, stored under the infra-red lamp. Cut small lumps of sugar with scissors and roll into balls. Push the top of a biro pen into the sugar to form a small hole, then attach a 3–5 mm gauge tube and seal. Start blowing gently near the infra-red lamp, rotating the tube and sugar; move in front of a fan and continue blowing gently until the cherry size is attained. Allow to cool completely, then cut off the surplus sugar and tube using a warm knife. Smooth the surface and form an indentation using the tip of a biro pen. Lay the cherry on silicone paper. Repeat the process for the second cherry. Both cherries must be the same size. Stick the cherries together and attach a very thin thread of green sugar on each cherry to form the stem. Shade with brown.

Blowing other shapes

VASE

There are many types of blown vases or similar items, all following similar basic princi-

ples. Prepare the sugar following the instructions described in the sugar pulling section (page 32).

The colour used can vary enormously, depending on what the vase is to be used for. If it is used for presenting flowers, then a contrast is necessary. A multi-coloured vase or a marbled pattern can be very effective when the flowers are all of one shade, or if the vase is exhibited as an item in itself.

> **Equipment**
> *Marble slab*
> *Sugar boiler*
> *Palette knife*
> *Large knife*
> *Metal scraper*
> *Thermometer*
> *Containers for lemon juice and oil*
> *Scissors*
> *Blowing tubes/hand pump (8 mm gauge)*
> *Fan*
> *Alcohol burner*
> *Hair drier*
> *Rolling pin*

To achieve an even mixture of colours in a marbled pattern, use equal quantities of pulled sugar in two shades and one-eighth in a much darker shade. Roll the three shades into a long sausage shape and, keeping it under the lamp, twist round continuously as if forming a rope, then fold over into a cylinder. This should now be ready for blowing into the required shape. Avoid mixing further, as this will spoil the pattern of colours. If the sugar has cooled too much for blowing, just allow it to sit in the storage tin under the infra-red lamp to soften.

The blowing technique for producing vase-type items is not much different from any other kind of pulled blowing. Using the foot pump for blowing a large vase or any large items would be difficult as the pump has to rest on the table, so either use the hand pump or blow by mouth.

Using un-pulled sugar: The vase can also look very effective if blown using un-pulled sugar. It requires some practice to master the technique, as the sugar is much hotter and less pliable than when it is pulled, but the translucent effect can be effective for these items. Pour the boiled sugar onto the oiled marble slab and allow to settle for a few minutes, then, using a large scraper, gently fold the edges towards the middle. Allow to stand for a few minutes then repeat the process once or twice more, until the sugar attains a firmer texture. It can then be picked up – surgical gloves can be useful. Attach the sugar to the blowing tube and follow the procedures as for pulled sugar blowing. Note that the sugar must not be stirred, as it would lose its transparent appearance.

Using pulled sugar: Prepare the pulled and coloured sugar (500 g cube sugar should be sufficient to produce a vase 18–20 cm high and 12 cm wide). Store the sugar in a large container under the infra-red lamp. Make sure it is evenly malleable, so that it will expand uniformly when blown.

As this item has to be blown to a larger shape, the hole in the sugar can be made using the oiled end of a rolling pin – the size of the hole depends on the size of the vase you intend to produce. Once a cylindrical hole is formed, remove the rolling pin immediately and attach the blowing tube; seal well. Start blowing softly and evenly, keeping under the infra-red lamp. Continually rotate the tube and sugar until the air has filled two-thirds of the cylinder. Do not disturb the end of the sugar at this stage, and keep blowing as evenly as possible.

It is also important to avoid the formation of creases and fingermarks while blowing;

surgical gloves help, but rotating the item is essential. As the air expands inside the sugar, run the palm of the hand over the lower half of the vase to form a concave shape, or any other shape desired. Running the edge of a palette knife about 4–5 cm from the base marks the base very efficiently. Use the fan when necessary to cool the vase and continue blowing, holding the vase in a perpendicular position above the marble slab and in front of the fan. Gently allow the vase to lengthen to the desired height. As the end of the cylinder begins to expand, allow the bottom to touch the surface of the marble slab. Rotating the vase in front of the fan, form a semi-flat base which will enable the vase to stand after it is completed.

With the vase held upright, allow it to cool completely in front of the fan. As the blowing reaches completion stage, the sugar will have to be cut at the top end and an opening made about 8–10 cm wide. Tie a string just below the position to be cut, as a guide. Then, using a warm knife, cut the sugar just above the string, making sure the heated sugar does not run down the outside of the vase and spoil the appearance.

Completion of the vase: The vase can be finished in many ways. For example, the opening can be curved outwards by heating it with the hair drier – gently blow warm air over the edge, while curving the sugar gently and gradually. Set into shape by quickly blowing cold air on it. The rim can also be finished by placing a small rope on the top and at the base. A handle, or two, can be placed on the side, again matching the rope. Stand the completed vase on a sugar base, for presentation.

BOWL

The techniques used are similar to those employed in blowing a vase. Colour the sugar as desired and, once pulled, store the sugar under the infra-red lamp. Using the procedure described earlier (page 47), blow softly while rotating the tube and sugar evenly until the air has filled three-quarters of the cylinder. Do not handle the solid sugar at the end of the cylinder while blowing, and do not allow the cylinder to lengthen before the air chamber has finished expanding.

When the cylinder is almost the right size, cool the sugar by standing it in front of the fan. When the sugar is completely cold, cut a lid shape off the end attached to the tube, using a warm knife. Remove the tube, cut off the surplus sugar, and smooth the top with a hot knife.

The lid can be used as the lid of the bowl,

decorated with a flower and leaves, or it can be turned over and used as the base for the bowl. With a piped sugar handle, the bowl can be a small, attractive centrepiece, ideal for petits fours.

SWAN

A blown sugar swan can provide a sublime finishing touch to an elegant banquet table. When prepared on a smaller scale and filled with mousse or sorbet, it serves as an exquisite dessert dish that would make a stunning table presentation.

Preparation: Boil the sugar using the usual recipe and method (see page 14). As the sugar

Blown sugar swans

needs to look white for the swan, it is essential to observe the correct temperature (152°C). As the sugar approaches this temperature, remove the pan from the heat and place the bottom in a container of iced water to stop the boiling process immediately. No added colour is necessary. Pour the sugar onto a lightly oiled marble slab and allow to settle for a few minutes. Using a metal scraper, fold in the edges towards the centre. Continue the folding technique until the solution thickens and has a malleable texture. Lift the mass of sugar with both hands. Holding the sugar with one hand, stretch it out with the other then re-join the mass. Repeat this operation 10–12 times, or until the mass of sugar has a high, glossy shine and is still completely pliable. Divide the sugar in half and store both pieces under the infra-red lamp.

Blowing procedure: Using the procedure described on page 47, blow softly while evenly rotating the blowing tube and sugar until the air chamber has filled two-thirds of the cylinder. At this stage it is important not to allow the cylinder to become too large too quickly. Stretch the cylinder to a large egg shape, keeping the work continuously under the infra-red lamp, and avoiding any creases being formed at the end of the blowing tube. At the same time, pull out the far end of the cylinder with a steady movement, extending it to about 20 mm, and immediately curve this over to form the shape of a swan's neck. While blowing, wrap your fingers round the end to form the head and squeeze the tip to make the beak. Taking care to keep the neck in the intended shape, move in front of the fan to cool the neck and head. Continue blowing the body part, holding it on the open palm of the hand, until it reaches the required size and shape. Avoid any further blowing unless needed to remove unwanted indentations or finger-marks. Allow to cool completely, then store upright using soft material such as tissues for support. You may prefer to position the swan immediately on a base, using a small piece of soft sugar to weld it on. Various bases can be used, such as a flat poured base or a poured base shaped to simulate a lake, adding water lilies and leaves, accompanied by spun sugar to enhance the display.

Making the wings and feathers: The wings can also be blown and kept flat. Shape them in proportion to the size of the body, making sure one curves to the left and one to the right. When cold, the wings can be attached to each side of the body, using a small piece of soft sugar or heating the base of the wing over a small flame.

The wings can also be made by pulling the sugar to various lengths as for the ribbon (see page 44). Quickly attach them to each other at the base, like a fan, again with one curved to the left and one to the right. Attach them at the base of the body, placed upright and partly open. The feathers are produced by pulling a small amount of sugar similar to leaves (see page 35). Heat the base of the feather over a small flame and attach it to the body, starting at the rear of the swan. Only 5–6 feathers are necessary to produce authenticity. The beak can be coloured deep red, using a small paint brush.

■ ROYAL ICING

Royal icing is a type of meringue (the heaviest form).

1 It should be capable of forming a peak with a fine point.
2 It should be light but *not* fluffy.
3 It should possess a pearly sheen, as does meringue.

Ingredients

Using fresh eggs:

Egg whites	$2\frac{1}{2}$–3
Icing sugar	500 g
Lemon juice	$\frac{1}{2}$ teaspoon

Using pure albumen or substitutes:

Albumen powder	15 g
Water	150 ml
Icing sugar	1 kg
Lemon juice	$\frac{1}{2}$ teaspoon

Types of albumen

Fresh egg: Not used to any large extent today – must be yolk free. Should be sieved. Should be allowed to stand to increase acidity.

Frozen egg: Better than above but usually requires acid to help beating qualities.

Dried egg: Soak for 15–20 minutes at least, preferably overnight, and strain before use. Use 1–$1\frac{1}{2}$ parts albumen to 10 of water.

Types of sugar

Several grades of icing sugar are available, but only good quality sugar should be used for royal icing. Store in moisture proof containers or bags. A small quantity of blue colouring gives a whiter appearance to royal icing. Do not use this, however, if any other colouring is to be added.

Method

Scald all utensils with boiling water, as the smallest amount of grease will prevent the icing reaching a stiff consistency.

Place the egg whites or diluted albumen in the mixing bowl, adding a touch of blue to enhance the appearance. Add the icing sugar (sieved if necessary) and mix to a smooth paste, using a clean spoon. Transfer to a food processor and beat at low speed until the icing stands in firm pointed peaks which retain their shape. Add the lemon juice while beating. Do not over-beat, as this will result in fluffy icing which gives a bubbly or rough surface if used for coating and causes frequent breaks when used for piping, due to the many air pockets. Having prepared the royal icing, scrape down the sides of the bowl immediately and cover the bowl with a damp cloth. This cloth must not be allowed to dry or a crust will form on the surface of the icing, making it unusable. If needed for coating, royal icing should be left to stand overnight, covered. When using, work the icing slowly with a spoon or palette knife to remove any air bubbles.

Piping techniques

Equipment

Piping tubes
Mixing bowl
Palette knife
Tablespoon
Scissors
Greaseproof paper cornet bags or piping bags
Plastic scraper

Begin by making contact with the object you wish to pipe on. Squeeze gently at first to gain control of the bag. Continue squeezing and, at the same time, raise the bag and pull it towards you. Once piping has begun, try to maintain a sagging line. Do not be afraid to lift the tube once piping has begun. When you are near the end of the line you should stop all pressure and carefully lower your hand back to the surface. Constant practice will enable you to start and finish at a specified point and to pipe in straight lines or any other shape. Continue piping other lines close to (but not touching) the preceding ones.

After practising, change to smaller tubes and repeat the exercise. Draw a stencil of a simple pattern with curves, and place this on a practice board as a guide. Pipe the curves as previously described for lines, but following the shape of the curves. Lower the tube and stop at the end of each curve, making a fresh start for the next curve. Take great care to see that the joins are neat and well defined.

Remove the stencil when completed and continue to pipe additional curves each side of the original pattern. Change the tubes again and practise as before. After a little progress has been made, you will acquire the habit of lifting the tube well clear of the board or object you are piping on. Continue to practise with different shapes of tubes to get the desired effect and to learn to control the pressure on the piping bag.

2 PETITS FOURS AND FRIANDISES

■ INTRODUCTION

The first sweetmeats were made of fruit preserves, using honey. Recipes for these can be traced back as far as Greek and Roman times. Later, in the Middle Ages, sticks of candy and sugar fancies were available for children, as sugar became cheaper. A further development was coating seeds, spices and fruits in hard sugar syrup. These were mainly sold by pedlars.

Confectioners and pâtissiers introduced the term petits fours in the early 18th century. *Petit* means small and *four* means oven or bakehouse. Petits fours are cakes or biscuits which can be consumed in one or two mouthfuls. They should be approximately $2\frac{1}{2}$–3 cm. All *petits fours glacés* should be served in paper cases, except biscuits and pastilles. Petits fours can be divided into three categories: *sec* (dry), *glacé* (glazed) and *varié* (assorted confectionery).

Petits fours sec are also used as decoration or served with ice creams, fruit salads, fruit fools, sabayons, coupes, etc.

Petits fours glacés and *variés* are usually referred to as *friandises* and these are ideal for displaying on a cold buffet or served with coffee at the end of dinners, parties or any elegant function. Variety and small quantities are important: two per person is the average.

Petits fours are made from the following:

Sec

1 Biscuits
2 Meringues
3 Almond mixing
4 Puff paste
5 Sweet paste

ALTERNATIVE TERMS		
Menu description	Meaning	On which menu
Petits fours	Small baked biscuits	General services
Friandises	Small sweet delicacies	Class functions
Gourmandise	Greediness (of tit-bits)	Gourmet evening
Sucrerie	Sweet candy	Ladies/children functions
Délice des dames	Ladies' delight	Ladies evenings
Mignardises	Small delicacies	General services
Les douceurs fines	Sweet finesse	Ladies evenings
Les frivolités gourmandes	Greed for frivolities	Gentlemen evenings
Corbeille d'excellence	Basket of excellence	High class service
Les frivolités	Bits and pieces	Happy time functions
Délice de la famille	Delights of the family	Family gatherings
Amuse gueules	Amuse your trap (mouth)	Fun/special evenings

Friandises glacés

1 Any under *sec*, with the addition of fondant or cream
2 Choux paste, addition of fondant or caramel
3 Genoise, addition of fondant, jam/jellies
4 Tartlets/barquettes, addition of fondant
5 Japonaise, addition of fondant, jam, caramel
6 Caramelised or dipped fruits

Alternative components of friandises

1 Fondant: coconut kisses, fudge
2 Jellies: marshmallow, Turkish delights
3 Chocolate: truffles, liqueurs, nuts
4 Marzipan: déguisés, fruits, figures
5 Sugar: toffees, fudges, nougat, pastilles
6 Fruits: dipped oranges or grapes, confits

■ PETITS FOURS GLACÉS

The very small fondant-covered articles known as *petits fours glacés* are generally made with a base consisting either of small pieces of a sponge (using a victoria or *Pain-de-Gênes* mix, or even a shortbread mix) or small pieces of dry sponge biscuits. For covering or sandwiching together, richly flavoured almond paste, butter creams, or chopped preserved fruits are mostly used. Various liqueurs are used for flavouring.

To finish, the petits fours are masked entirely with fondant and placed in small fancy crimped paper cases. They should then be decorated, either with a light scroll piped on with fondant or by placing some chopped or split pistachio nuts, crystallised flowers or chopped preserved fruits in the centre.

Pain de Gênes

Ingredients	
Butter	250 g
Caster sugar	500 g
Eggs	10
Ground almonds	250 g
Flour	250 g
Liqueur to taste (optional)	

Cream the butter and sugar. Add the eggs gradually and continue beating until the mixture is light and fluffy. Add the liqueur, if required, and mix well. Fold in the flour and ground almonds. Avoid over-mixing. Spread an even layer, about 10 mm thick, in a paper-lined, greased swiss roll tin. Bake at 204°C. Melted couverture, coffee flavour, or other flavour and colour can be added to the basic recipe during the creaming stage to obtain a nice colour. The sponge will be very fragile when removed from the oven: allow to cool for about 10 minutes, then turn out onto greaseproof paper and allow to get cold. If the sponge is to be stored, wrap well in polythene bags and store flat in the refrigerator or freezer. Do not store sponges on top of each other or place other items on top.

Coating with fondant

Place the prepared sponge on a sheet of greaseproof paper and remove the top, if necessary, using a long sharp serrated knife. Roll out sufficient marzipan to cover the slab of sponge, about 3 mm thick. Brush all over the marzipan with boiled apricot jam then place the prepared sponge on top and, using a brush, moisten with stock syrup and liqueur. If required, spread an even layer of flavoured butter cream on the sponge, then place the second layer of sponge on top. Place a flat tray on top and press to even the surface.

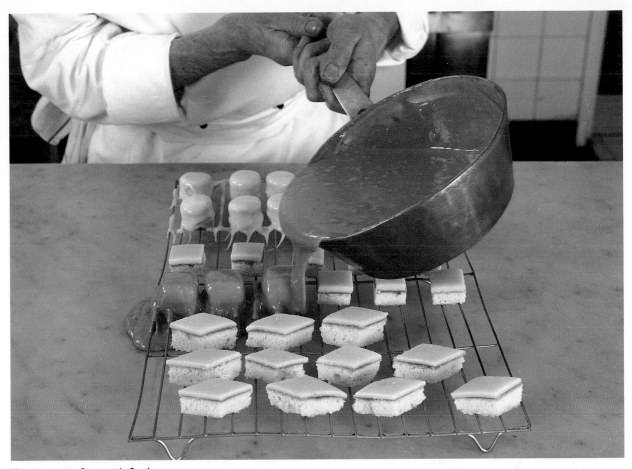

Coating petits fours with fondant

The sponge is now ready for cutting as required: use small fancy cutters or a large knife. Uniformity is very important as the petits fours are so small. Place the cut pieces about 20 mm apart on a wire tray, on a clean surface, with the marzipan uppermost. Prepare the fondant (see page 27), preferably using a sauteuse. It can be coloured and flavoured as desired, but be sure to keep to pastel shades. Melted couverture can be used for flavouring and colouring, but it may then be necessary to thin the fondant with extra syrup, as the chocolate will act as a thickening agent. The fondant temperature is important as, if too hot, the fondant will lose its gloss and become hard and brittle. Add a little stock syrup to

attain a nice flowing consistency, not too thick or too soft. Experiment with a single piece first. A small amount of stock syrup or a touch of egg white will encourage the development of gloss on the fondant. Beat the fondant well, then, holding the sauteuse tilted towards you, use a large metal spoon to coat the fondant pieces in one go, completing one row at a time. If the process is repeated it will increase the thickness and spoil the appearance.

An alternative technique of pouring the fondant directly over the petits fours is practised by many professional confectioners and pâtissiers. Although some practice is required, the technique can produce effective results. Holding the sauteuse with two hands, move

A selection of fondant-covered petits fours

from top right to left, covering one row of petits fours in one go without stopping. The sauteuse, being wider than the spoon, will coat the pieces with ease. Once the batch is complete, remove the wire tray, scrape the fondant off the table and put this back in the sauteuse for further use.

Pipe attractive fine patterns on top of the petits fours, using a paper cornet filled with fondant. Complete by adding small decorations, such as angelica, glacé cherries, mimosa, crystallised violets and rose petals. Allow the glazed petits fours to set, then loosen with a wet palette knife and place each one in a paper case for serving.

The remaining fondant can be used again. Scrape the sides of the saucepan down and cover with cold water; when re-using, pour out the water and warm again to a flowing consistency.

Colouring

The fondant can be coloured and flavoured as required, using good quality liquid food colours. Always add colouring to the fondant a little at a time. If too much is added, it cannot be changed. Pastel shades always look more appealing and attractive on the dish. Three colours can be easily obtained from the same batch of fondant, as follows:

1 Use the white fondant as the first colour.
2 Add yellow to the white fondant for the second colour.
3 Add red to the yellow fondant to make orange – the third colour.

Couverture could be added to the remainder of the orange, to obtain a fourth colour.

Rich almond paste petits fours

Rich almond paste petits fours can be made by placing a thick layer of almond paste in place of the second layer of sponge, then proceeding as before.

Barquettes glacées

Ingredients
Sweet paste
Raspberry jam
Frangipane
Apricot jam
Fondant
Decorations

Equipment
Bowl for dusting flour
Rolling pins (two)
Barquette moulds (5 cm)
Sauteuse for fondant
Spatula
Paper comets (two)
Baking tray

Arrange the barquette moulds close together on the working surface. Roll the sweet paste thinly (2 mm). Roll the paste over the rolling pin and unwind it over the prepared moulds. Using a small lump of paste, preferably puff paste trimmings, line the mould by pressing the paste gently into them. Roll two rolling pins held close to each other over the moulds to cut off the surplus paste. Place the moulds on a clean surface, then using a paper cornet filled with raspberry jam, pipe a small amount on the base of each lined mould. Spread the frangipane in each mould with a small palette knife, filling it flat to the rim. Place on a clean tray and bake at 204°C.

Once baked, immediately turn the barquettes over onto a surface lined with greaseproof paper, leaving the moulds on them. This will provide a flat surface which is very useful for decorating. Brush the surface of the barquettes with boiled apricot jam and allow to set. Using a sauteuse, prepare the fondant as previously described. Colour and flavour as required. Place the sauteuse on a damp cloth, tilting towards you. Holding the base of the barquette, dip the top into the fondant, lift, and immediately wipe the surplus fondant using the forefinger or the end of a small knife. Allow to set. Decorate the tops by piping a fine thread of fondant, coloured as desired. Complete by adding other decorations, such as small pieces of angelica, glacé cherries, mimosa, crystallised violets and rose petals. Place the petits fours in paper cases for serving.

Tartelettes glacées

Equipment
Bowl for dusting flour
Rolling pin
Cutters (2½–3 cm)
Piping bag
Paper cornets (two)
Sauteuse for fondant
Spatula
Baking tray

Use the same ingredients and follow the same procedure as for the barquettes, but cut the paste using the cutters and place them in each mould. Shape the paste well so that it reaches just above the rim. Pipe the raspberry jam into the bases, using the piping bag nearly filled with frangipane. Bake and complete as for the barquettes glacées.

Friands

Ingredients	
Ground almonds	125 g
Caster sugar	125 g
Butter (melted)	60 g
Flour	20 g
Egg whites	3

Mix together the ground almonds, sugar, butter and flour in a bowl. Add the egg whites and mix well together. Fill well-greased barquette moulds, 2½–3 cm in size, and flatten the tops with a palette knife. Bake at 204°C. When baked, turn upside down onto greaseproof paper (to flatten the tops) and allow to get cold.

Decorate the tops as for barquettes and tartelettes, or just dredge with icing sugar and glaze under the salamander.

Liqueurs bonbons

Ingredients	
Cube or granulated sugar	I kg
Water	3 dl
Liqueur of choice	

Prepare the specially made starch trays (3 cm deep trays filled with cornflour). Make impressions in the cornflour using a row of forms attached to a wooden rod the size of the starch tray; each form is about 20 mm in diameter and 10 mm deep. Make sure the impressions are regular, in rows 10 mm apart from each other. Make as many as possible in one tray.

Place the sugar in a clean sugar boiler, add the water and dissolve slowly. At the boiling stage, increase the heat and boil briskly until the density reaches 34° Baumé. It is advisable to test the syrup with the saccharometer if liqueurs are to be added. Continue boiling to increase the density further to 36° Baumé, then continue boiling until the syrup reaches 37° Baumé. Flavour and colour can be added just before this density is reached.

To fill the impressions, warm the filling funnel, place in the funnel stick and pour in the boiled solution to half full. By slightly raising the funnel stick, sufficient sugar is allowed to flow out into each impression. The solution should be quickly used while hot, to prevent it from setting firm in the funnel. When the starch tray is complete, place in a warm (not hot) drying cupboard for a few hours (a dry warm place or prover would suffice).

Fondant can also be used for the production of bonbons; just heat sufficient fondant in a saucepan gently, then boil to 34° Baumé or 110°C.

Crystallising bonbons: Produce a syrup by boiling 6 dl of water with 500 g of cube or granulated sugar. Make sure the saucepan is clean and free from grease or any undissolved sugar crystals which can cause re-crystallisation of the syrup. Continue boiling until the density reaches 31° Baumé. Partly cover with a lid and store to cool or until required.

For dipping the bonbons follow the procedure described below.

Crystallising fondants: Remove the fondants from the starch and brush with a soft brush to remove any remaining cornflour. Pack them close together in deep trays and cover with a wire tray – this is to keep them on the base when flooded with the syrup. Do not agitate the syrup at this stage: use a ladle to pour the syrup over the fondants. It should not be drawn from the sides of the saucepan as any vibration is likely to cause the syrup to grain and set firm. When all the fondants are covered, store until the following day, covered with a tray on top. Gently pour out the surplus syrup, tilting the tray. Carefully lift out the fondants and neatly place on a fine wire tray. Store in a warm place until quite dry; the surface should have a covering of fine, bright, sugar crystals.

Dipped fruits

Ingredients

Cube or granulated sugar	500 g
Liquid glucose	50 g
Water	100 ml

Equipment

Sugar boiler
Triangle
Damp cloth
Tweezers
Dipping fork
Dry cloth
Bowl for the oil
Draining wire

PREPARATION

Follow the techniques described in sugar boiling (page 14), ensuring that all utensils are clean and free from grease.

The fruit to be dipped has to be allowed to dry for at least one hour in a warm place (on top of the oven); oranges and grapes could be prepared on the previous day. A marble slab is ideal as a surface, but an oiled tray (not greased) would do very well. The advance preparation of the table (*mise-en-scène*) with utensils, etc., is essential. Place the triangle on the table, covered with the damp cloth: this will prevent the saucepan sliding about on the table. Always place the saucepan with the handle turned away from the front. Have the fruit on the left side and the dipping fork and tweezers on the right side; the oiled surface should also be on the left.

Technique: Boil the sugar as described in the sugar boiling section (page 14), observing the necessary precautions. When the sugar reaches 153°C, remove from the heat using a dry cloth, and place on the work surface.

Use the tweezers for grapes, cherries and strawberries, the dipping fork for oranges, mandarins, marzipan and déguisés. Ensure that all dipped items are completely coated with the boiled sugar.

1   Pick up the fruit with the tweezers, dip into the sugar, wipe off surplus on the edge of the saucepan and quickly place on the oiled surface.
2   Drop the fruit or déguisé into the boiled sugar, lift out with the dipping fork, wipe the base on the edge of the saucepan and place on the oiled surface.
3   Allow the fruit to cool completely. Trim the stems of the grapes if necessary and place in paper cases for serving. Dipping should not be done more than two hours before serving. *Do not* puncture the fruit, as the

acid of the juices weeping out will crystal-lise the sugar while dipping.

STRAWBERRIES

Select fresh, uniformly-shaped strawberries and allow to dry, gently wrapped in a soft cloth. Hold the fruit by the calyx for dipping and place on icing sugar to dry. Strawberries are very attractive when dipped in semi-hot fondant.

GRAPES

Select good quality fruit, either black or white grapes. Divide small- or medium-sized grapes into pairs; cut large grapes singly. Dip using tweezers.

Dip small grapes in pairs

ORANGES

Slit the surface of the skin using the point of a small knife and place the whole fruit in boiling water; leave on medium heat until the cut grooves begin to show signs of opening. Place quickly in cold water and allow to cool. Remove the skin, ensuring that the white pith is also removed, without damaging the orange.

Separate into segments and place them on a wire tray to dry. The orange segments can be dipped holding one end between thumb and

forefinger; dip half the segment, allow to set, then dip the other half in a different coloured sugar.

Dip oranges using a dipping fork

MANDARINS

The skin of these fruits is loose and softer than the orange, so it will not be necessary to place them in hot water first as the skin can be removed easily.

ALMONDS

Use blanched almonds, placing three or four almonds together. Dip using the dipping fork.

CHERRIES

Select good quality fruit. Do not remove the stalks and keep the pairs attached. Do not remove the stone, as the cherry juice will crystallise the sugar.

RED/BLACKCURRANTS

Select good quality fruit. Wash them well and allow to dry in a sieve. Dip them in the boiled sugar, holding the stalks. These soft fruits are better placed on a sheet of waxed paper when dipped.

PISTACHIO

Prepare green-coloured pistachio-flavoured marzipan and form into small balls. Place 6–8 blanched and skinned pistachio nuts round each ball. Allow to dry. Dip in boiled sugar and complete by placing a pistachio nut on top.

A selection of dipped centres: fruits and déguisés

Marzipan friandises *(déguisés)*

These friandises are made with dried or crystallised fruits which are stuffed or coated with marzipan. This can be coloured and flavoured, and fruits can be mixed into the marzipan.

CHESTNUTS
Use chestnut purée, or push cooked chestnuts through a fine sieve. Mix in a little butter, rum, and an equal quantity of marzipan. Form into equal-shaped balls and place on a paper-lined tray. Set firm in the refrigerator then dip in boiled sugar using the dipping fork.

PRUNES
Because of their natural black colour, this fruit will look attractive using either pink or green-coloured marzipan. Cut the fruit in half and discard the stone. Roll the marzipan into a sausage shape and cut into equal-sized pieces. Form into balls and squeeze a marzipan ball into the cavity of each half prune. Allow the marzipan to dry well, then dip in the boiled sugar using the dipping fork.

DATES
Follow the same technique as for the prunes. Yellow colouring would be more suitable.

CHERRIES
Cut glacé cherries in half. Roll the marzipan into a sausage shape, cut into equal-sized pieces and form into balls. Place a half cherry on either side of a ball and re-form into a ball. Allow to dry before dipping in boiled sugar using the dipping fork.

WALNUTS
Mix one-third crushed walnuts to one quantity of marzipan. Roll into a sausage shape, cut into equal-sized pieces and form into balls. Place one half walnut on top and allow to dry. Dip in boiled sugar using the dipping fork.

HAZELNUTS
Mix one-third of ground hazelnuts to one quantity of marzipan. Roll into a sausage shape, cut into equal-sized pieces and form into balls. Insert a skinned hazelnut in the centre of each marzipan ball and re-form. Allow to dry. Dip in boiled sugar using the dipping fork and immediately place another skinned hazelnut on top.

Selection of classic fondant-coated petits fours

ADMIRAL
Sandwich together layers of almond-flavoured sponge or Pain-de-Gênes with orange-

flavoured butter cream. Brush with boiled apricot jam, cover with a thin layer of marzipan and coat with orange-flavoured fondant. Decorate.

ABYSSINIA
Sandwich together layers of almond-flavoured sponge with praline-flavoured butter cream. Brush with boiled apricot jam, then cover with a thin layer of marzipan. Coat with pineapple-flavoured fondant and decorate the top with crystallised pineapple.

CAROLINE
Fill small eclairs, 20 cm in length, with chocolate-flavoured butter cream or crème pâtissière. Coat with chocolate-flavoured fondant.

COLOMBOS
Fill small choux buns with vanilla-flavoured crème pâtissière. Dip the tops in light caramel and place an almond on top.

CARNIVAL HAT
Mound a small amount of strawberry jam on a baked round shortbread biscuit. Glaze with white fondant. Decorate with crystallised violets.

CHOUX MAXIM
Fill a small choux bun with curacao-flavoured crème pâtissière. Coat with orange-flavoured fondant and decorate with chocolate fondant.

DOMINOES
Sandwich almond biscuit with vanilla butter cream and cut into oblong shapes. Glaze with white fondant. Decorate, simulating the domino pattern on top.

DIANE
Fill small choux buns with rum-flavoured crème pâtissière and coat with pink-coloured

fondant. Decorate with crystallised rose.

FROG'S HEAD
Using a plain tube, pipe plain butter cream over a half macaroon to form a half ball. Coat completely with green-coloured fondant and allow to set. Use a small wet knife to cut out a small wedge for the mouth of the frog. Decorate with chocolate to represent the eyes and eyebrows.

GANACHE
Bake a small round chocolate-flavoured shortbread biscuit; brush with boiled apricot jam and pipe on a rosette of rum- and chocolate-flavoured butter cream. Chill, then coat with chocolate-flavoured fondant.

HARLEQUIN
Sandwich together layers of chocolate sponge, moistened with syrup or rum, with vanilla-flavoured butter cream. Brush over with boiled apricot jam and cover with a thin layer of marzipan. Coat half with chocolate and half with vanilla fondant.

JAPONAISE
Sandwich two almond meringue biscuits together with rum- and praline-flavoured butter cream. Coat the tops with green-coloured fondant and decorate with a pistachio nut.

JAVANAISE
Sandwich almond biscuits with coffee butter cream and coat the top with coffee-flavoured and coloured fondant.

MONTMORENCY
Bake an almond-flavoured biscuit. Place a mound of raspberry jam in the centre and arrange three poached cherries on top. Glaze with kirsch-flavoured fondant.

METEORS

Sandwich together two macaroon biscuits with raspberry jam and raspberry-flavoured butter cream. Set in the refrigerator, then coat with raspberry-flavoured fondant. Place a crystallised rose on top.

MALAKOFF

Prepare small frangipane barquettes and brush boiled apricot jam on top. Coat with coffee-flavoured fondant and decorate with a marzipan coffee bean.

NAPOLITAINE

Sandwich two layers of sponge, one pink and one green, with pistachio-flavoured plain butter cream. Cut oblong shapes and coat with white fondant. Place an almond on top.

ROYAL

Make small biscuit bases and pipe with a raised praline-flavoured butter cream ring. Fill the centre with redcurrant jelly. Glaze by sprinkling white fondant on top.

ROGNONS (KIDNEYS)

Bake half-moon-shaped almond biscuits and sandwich with raspberry jam and raspberry-flavoured butter cream. Coat with chocolate-flavoured fondant and decorate with a half almond on top.

Crystallised candies (Sucre candi)

Arab countries were the original producers of sweets using crystallisation techniques; they were called *Qand*, translated as cane. The Italian explorer, Marco Polo, introduced these crystallised sweets into Europe and named them candy. Crystallisation is merely a way of preserving by using sugar syrup.

Marzipan friandises: All marzipan and fruit déguisés can be processed for crystallisation.

Follow the instructions described in the crystallisation of bonbons (page 62).

CRYSTALLISATION OF FRUITS

Fruit confits: The most suitable fruits are those which have a positive flavour and a firm texture. All fruits used should be slightly under-ripe and unblemished. ·

Pears Apples	Peeled, cut in half or quarters (sprinkled with lemon juice to stop discolouring)
Mandarins Oranges	Segmented, pith removed (two together if small)
Peaches	Peeled by blanching, cut in half or quarters
Plums Greengage	Skin left on, pricked all over with a fork
Pineapple	Sliced in rings

Ingredients: Syrup	
Sugar	*1 kg*
Water	*1 litre*

Technique

1 Place the washed fruit in a saucepan of cold water and bring to the boil; simmer gently for a few minutes keeping the fruit moving.

2 Refresh well under cold running water: this removes the tannin and malic acid which would cause the fruit to blacken eventually.

3 Place the fruit in a copper basin and cover with boiling syrup at 18° Baumé. Bring back to simmering point, store in a cool place.

4 After two days drain off the syrup from the fruit, being careful not to damage the fruit.

5 After draining the syrup measure the amount in litres and raise it by 2° Baumé. Add 60 g of sugar for every 1 litre of syrup.

6 Bring the syrup to the boil to dissolve the sugar, then carefully add in the fruit and bring back to simmering point. Place in a container and leave for another two days.

7 Repeat this procedure every two days until 34° Baumé is reached and add 100 g of glucose to every 1 litre of syrup.

8 Leave in the container for two weeks.

9 Raise the syrup to 36° Baumé, repeating step 6. Place in the container and allow to get cold. Cover and store in a cool place and use as required. The syrup may be used as flavouring.

To serve as friandises: Drain the fruit well over a clean sieve or wire. Cut in sections and roll in caster sugar. Place in paper cases for serving.

GLAZED CHESTNUTS (MARRONS GLACÉS)

Ingredients	
Chestnuts	I kg
Cube sugar	2 kg
Glucose	250 g
Vanilla flavour	
Water	I litre

Italian chestnuts are the best for size and quality. Place in boiling water for 4–5 minutes, drain and rinse under cold water, then gently remove the skins without damaging the kernel. Place the chestnuts in a cloth and rub together to remove the remaining brownish skin. Place the skinned chestnuts in boiling water again to simmer for about one hour or until they are slightly tender when tested with a small knife. Proceed as described in the crystallisation of fruits (page 67). Any damaged chestnuts can be covered with melted couverture and rum and formed into balls similar to truffles.

LEMON AND ORANGE PEEL

This peel can be used, and should not be wasted. Discard any not of good firm quality, then soak the peel for a few hours. Place in slightly salted water and boil for about half an hour. Rinse well under cold water. Continue, following the same process as for crystallisation of fruits (see page 67), but complete the process after four days (step 6). Store in sealed jars and use sliced as required: for decorating fruit dishes, coupes, ice-cream dishes, gâteaux, etc.

■ BOILED SUGAR PETITS FOURS
(PETITS FOURS AU SUCRE BOUILLI)

Caramels

SOFT CHOCLATE CARAMELS (CARAMEL MOUS AU CHOCOLAT)

Ingredients	
Cube sugar	250 g
Double cream	300 ml
Couverture (melted)	50 g
Glucose or honey	80 g

Place all the ingredients in a clean saucepan (not copper, as cream is being used). Boil over a high heat to 145°C, washing down the sides of the saucepan occasionally. Oil the marble slab and a 15 cm flan ring. Pour on the cooked mixture, allow to get completely cold, then cut into small cubes.

SOFT COFFEE CARAMELS (CARAMEL MOUS AU CAFÉ)

Proceed as for soft chocolate caramels, replacing the chocolate with concentrated coffee.

SOFT VANILLA CARAMELS (CARAMEL MOUS AU VANILLE)

Proceed as for soft chocolate caramels, replacing the chocolate with vanilla flavour. Add this when the sugar has reached the required temperature and stopped boiling.

HARD VANILLA CARAMELS (CARAMEL DURS AU VANILLE)

Ingredients	
Cube sugar	500 g
Glucose	250 g
Milk	300 ml
Double cream	300 ml
Butter	125 g
Vanilla to taste	

Melt the sugar in the milk over low heat until it becomes a syrup, then bring to the boil. Add the glucose and continue boiling up to 120°C. Add the cream gradually and continue boiling. Remove from the heat and add the butter and vanilla, stirring gently. Allow to continue boiling until it reaches 158°C. Pour the mixture onto an oiled marble slab, allow to just set, and cut into even-sized cubes. If it is possible to use cocoa butter instead of butter, the caramel will be much firmer.

HARD CHOCOLATE CARAMELS (CARAMEL DURS AU CHOCOLAT)

Proceed as for hard vanilla caramels, adding 200 g of melted couverture in place of the butter.

HARD COFFEE CARAMELS (CARAMEL DURS AU CAFÉ)

Proceed as for hard vanilla caramels, replacing the vanilla with concentrated coffee.

HARD HONEY CARAMELS (CARAMEL DURS AU MIEL)

Ingredients	
Cube sugar	500 g
Glucose	100 g
Honey	200 g
Condensed milk	500 g
Butter	125 g

Boil the sugar, honey, glucose and milk up to 120°C. Reduce the heat and gradually add the cream, stirring very gently. Add the butter and continue boiling to 158°C. Pour on an oiled marble slab, allow to become cold, then cut into the required shape.

BUTTERSCOTCH

Ingredients	
Cube sugar	750 g
Glucose	125 g
Butter	125 g
Water	400 ml
Lemon	1

Grate the lemon zest onto the sugar. Pour on the water and boil over low heat. Add the glucose. Once the sugar has dissolved, continue boiling fast to 130°C. Add the butter, stirring gently, and continue boiling until 140°C is reached. Turn the mixture onto an oiled marble slab, using an oiled flan ring. When set, cut to the desired shapes.

Fudge

This form of sweetmeat originated in the United States where it has achieved considerable popularity. It is said to have been made by girl students at one of the American universities, who gave the name 'fudge' to their invention.

Although the process of making fudge is simple, considerable care is needed to obtain a mass of the correct consistency.

Fudge is fundamentally a combination of caramel and fondant; it should have a fine-grain texture with a milky flavour. The graining may be produced by one of two methods, by agitation of the batch or by the introduction of fondant.

Points to observe

1 Cool the batch sufficiently before adding the fondant.
2 Do not pour a hot batch onto a cold slab.

Either of these will cause a coarse grain and a spotted appearance. The fudge mix should be poured into shallow wooden trays lined with waxed paper and left to set until the following day. The slabs should be marked and cut in squares, using a sharp damp knife. This form of confectionery lends itself admirably to a wide variety of flavours.

Ingredients	
Sugar	$1\frac{1}{2}$ kg
Sugar, brown	250 g
Glucose	2 kg
Condensed milk	1 kg
Water	600 ml
Butter	250 g
Fondant	1 kg

Boil the sugar, glucose and water to 135°C. Remove the pan from the heat, warm the butter and milk sufficiently to form a paste and stir this into the mixture. Return to the heat and boil to 118°C. Set aside to cool slightly, then stir in the fondant, broken in pieces, and any chosen flavour: chocolate, coffee, etc. Pour into the prepared tray, lined with waxed paper. When sufficiently cool, score divisions with a damp knife. Store, covered with paper, until the following day.

VANILLA FUDGE

Ingredients	
Soft brown sugar	1 kg
Condensed milk	1 kg
Glucose	500 g
Fondant	750 g
Vanilla flavour	
Butter	250 g

Using a copper saucepan, boil the sugar and glucose to 140°C, then add the butter, condensed milk and vanilla flavour. Pour into a paper-lined swiss roll tin and allow to set. Cut out the shapes required using a damp sharp knife. Place in paper cases for serving.

CHOCOLATE FUDGE
Proceed as for vanilla fudge, using sufficient melted couverture to obtain adequate colour and flavour.

COFFEE FUDGE
Proceed as for vanilla fudge, using sufficient coffee concentrate to obtain adequate colour and flavour.

BRAZIL NUT FUDGE
Proceed as for vanilla fudge, adding 150 g of skinned Brazil nuts just before pouring into the tin.

Candy cushions (Berlingots)

Boil the sugar, following the basic sugar boiling recipe (page 14). As soon as it reaches 154°C, remove from the heat and allow the bubbles to subside. Add 10 ml of pure lemon juice and any colour or flavour. Shake well and pour the mixture on an oiled marble slab. Wait a few minutes until it settles slightly, then fold in the edges. Repeat this again a few minutes later. At this stage the sugar should be sufficiently firm to lift with both hands. Stretch the sugar to twice its length then bring the ends together. Repeat this process about 6 times; the sugar at this stage should resemble a thick ribbon. Close in the pieces together to form a tube, keeping the air in. Pull the sugar again to double its length, fold again and continue until you have several tubes together. If possible the cushions should be cut immediately to the required size, using a sharp knife. Alternatively, the lengths can be allowed to get cold, then cut using an old knife heated and wiped with a damp cloth.

Nougat Montelimar

Ingredients	
Cube sugar	1 kg
Water	200 ml
Liquid glucose	250 g
Honey	200 g
Egg whites	120 g
Almonds	200 g
Pistachio nuts	200 g
Hazelnuts	200 g

Boil the sugar, following the basic sugar boiling recipe (page 14), add the liquid glucose and continue boiling to about 120°C. Add the honey and boil to 140°C. By this stage the egg whites should have been whisked until they stand in points. Using a mixer, gradually pour in the boiled sugar, while whisking, until all the boiled sugar and honey has been added. Replace the whisk with a beater and beat until nearly cold, at a slower speed. At the last stage, add the fruit and cherries; avoid mixing more than necessary.

Spread the mixture on rice paper and place another sheet of rice paper on top. Flatten, using a rolling pin, and allow to set. Cut to the required shapes when cold.

Peppermint pastilles *(Pastilles de menthe)*

Ingredients	
Cube sugar	500 g
Water	100 ml
Icing sugar	130 g
Oil of peppermint to taste	
Colour (optional)	

Boil the sugar following the basic sugar boiling recipe (page 14). When the sugar has reached 123°C, place the saucepan on a triangle. Allow the bubbles to subside, then stir in the icing sugar, peppermint and colour, using a whisk. Pour the mixture into a warm funnel. Holding the funnel in one hand, raise the funnel stick with the other and allow the mixture to drop evenly onto a clean marble slab (oil is not necessary as the sugar will contract on setting and is easily removed).

Note: Other flavours and colour can be used in place of the peppermint. The pastilles are normally placed on dishes without paper cases.

Marshmallow (1)

Ingredients	
Gum arabic	750 g
Cube sugar	750 g
Water	1 litre
Egg whites	150 ml
Glucose	250 g
Orange flower water	100 ml

Leave the gum to soak overnight in three-quarters of the water. This soaking will be greatly helped if warm water is used and the container is allowed to stand in a warm place, such as the prover. In the morning, boil the sugar with the remaining water, using a copper sugar boiler large enough to eventually take all the mixture. Add the glucose and boil to 123°C. The gum should be lightly warmed to dissolve, then added to the sugar solution with the orange flower water.

It is important that the egg whites are whisked while the sugar reaches the required temperature. While whisking, gradually add the boiled solution, as for making Italian meringue. Continue beating until the mass is white, light, and spongy. Place the mixture in swiss roll tins, lined with icing sugar. Cut this up when cold, using a damp knife, and roll in icing sugar. Place in paper cases for serving or dip in melted chocolate when set.

Marshmallow (2)

Ingredients	
Cube sugar	750 g
Water	600 ml
Egg whites	400 ml
Leaf gelatine	35 g
Cream of tartar	pinch
Flavour and colour as required (orange, lemon, peppermint, etc)	

Soak the gelatine with half of the water and place over a low heat to dissolve. Boil the sugar with the remaining water, adding a pinch of cream of tartar, until it reaches 130°C.

Meanwhile whisk the egg whites. When the sugar reaches the required temperature, pour gradually into the whisked egg whites, forming a light Italian meringue; continue whisking, adding flavour and colour as desired. Pour into swiss roll tins, allow to set. Complete as for previous recipe.

Turkish delight (Gelatine type)

Ingredients	
Cube sugar	I kg
Water	300 ml
Honey	150 g
Leaf gelatine	75 g
Flavour as required (orange, lemon, etc.)	

Soak the gelatine with the cold water. Boil the sugar to 110°C, using a copper sugar boiler sufficiently large to hold all the liquid. Add the honey and continue boiling to 123°C.

Warm the gelatine and water until it dissolves, then gradually pour into the boiled sugar. Add the flavour and colour. Pour the mixture into swiss roll tins and allow to set. To remove, lightly warm the base of the tin and turn the set mixture out onto a bed of icing sugar. With a damp knife, cut the delight to the required size and roll in plenty of icing sugar. Use paper cases for serving.

Turkish delight (Starchy type)

Ingredients	
Cube sugar	I kg 250 g
Leaf gelatine	60 g
Potato starch or arrowroot	125 g
Glucose	60 g
Flavour as required	

Dilute the starch with half the water, and use the remaining water to saturate the sugar. Boil to 123°C. Add the diluted starch mixture, flavour and colour; reboil and proceed as for previous recipe.

Caramel nougat (Croquante)

Elaborate pieces, recognised by confectioners and pâtissiers as pièces montées, have been widely used for many years, dating back as far

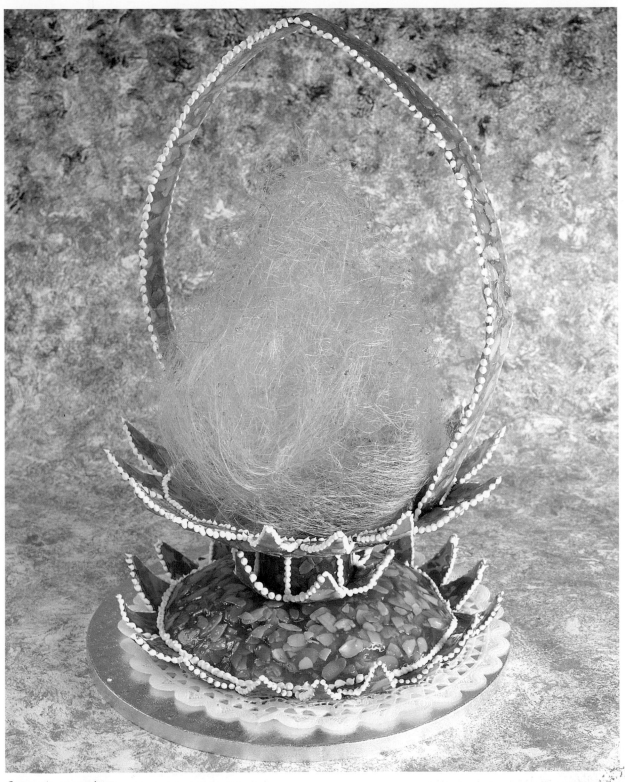

Croquante centrepiece

as Napoleonic times. At present, they are basically used as ornamental pieces in the form of stands or monumental shapes, on occasion representing household furniture or buildings. An original centrepiece can be made from nougat in the shape of the horn-of-plenty, ideal for presenting petits fours, flowers or sugar blown fruits and vegetables.

Unlike pulled sugar work, nougat can be eaten. As with many other confectionery works, it was introduced into England by the famous pâtissier Monsieur Antonin Carême. Besides being ornamental, nougat can be cut into pieces and served with petits fours. If ground into powder form, it is then recognised as praline, used in a wide variety of dishes: ice cream, butter cream for gâteaux and torten, sauces or mixed with crème pâtissière.

Ingredients

Cube or granulated sugar	500 g
Juice from one lemon	
Glucose	50 g
Chopped or flaked almonds	250 g
Butter for petits fours	100 g

Equipment

Oiled marble slab
Stencils or form
Sugar boiler or sauteuse
Spatula
Rolling pin
Saucepan stand
Large knife
Palette knife
Chopping board
Piping bag for royal icing

Prepare the working surface as described in the boiled sugar section (see page 14); cleanliness of all equipment is paramount. Ensure all equipment is at hand before beginning to boil the sugar.

It is essential to shake nibbed almonds (if used) over a sieve, to remove any dust particles which would crystallise the sugar prematurely. It is also important to warm all the almonds in the oven, on a paper-lined tray; if used cold they could encourage crystallisation. Stir the sugar and glucose in a copper boiler or sauteuse at low heat until well melted (or at least until the grains of sugar cannot be seen). If the sugar is soaked in water, the nougat would work but the flavour and texture would not be comparable.

It is a good idea to use a large sauteuse rather than a saucepan as it helps when mixing in the almonds, but be careful to keep the sugar in the centre. Avoid the sugar smearing the sides; wash down the sides occasionally using a clean brush dipped in cold water.

When the sugar comes to the boil increase to a high heat. If gas is being used make sure the flames are kept under the saucepan. Continue boiling until the sugar turns a golden chestnut-brown colour. Remove from the heat and stir in the warmed almonds, then return to a medium heat, stirring occasionally with a spatula. When the correct light-caramel colour is attained, the mixture can be poured onto the oiled marble slab or shaped form, previously prepared. Care is necessary to avoid over-cooking the mixture: if it is too dark it will not have the correct appearance and it will also have a bitter taste.

The poured nougat has to be allowed to form a skin on the surface – this happens within minutes of pouring – then, with the aid of a palette knife and metal scraper, lift the nougat and turn it over. The nougat can now be rolled out to obtain a thinner texture. If necessary, place the nougat on a baking sheet, either oiled or lined with silicone paper, and place in a medium warm oven for a few minutes to soften. When removed, it can be rolled out again to make it uniformly thinner, as required. A large chopping board is useful for rolling the nougat; a cold surface will cool the nougat too fast, making it difficult to roll and cut. The nougat can be put back in the oven as often as required, as long as the oven temperature never becomes hot.

Always use a large knife for cutting nougat, wiping it with a damp warm cloth each time. The cut pieces of nougat can be assembled as soon as possible, either by dipping the ends of pieces into boiled sugar to hard crack, or by melting the edges over a small flame until bubbles begin to appear; the pieces can then be attached together. Complete the ornament by piping a decoration with royal icing. You can also decorate with pulled sugar or marzipan flowers and leaves.

Note: For marzipan and chocolate petits fours, refer to chapters 4 and 5.

3 PASTILLAGE

■ INTRODUCTION

It was the French master confectioner and pâtissier Antonin Carême (1784–1833) who first introduced artistic masterpieces in pastillage and showed illustrations of his work in *Le Pâtissier Pittoresque* and *Pâtissier Royal*.

This was then followed by another great French pâtissier, Pierre Lacam, who in 1860 designed a selection of centrepieces accompanied by petits fours and sweets, particularly Italian meringue. Pierre Lacam published his work, in 1865, in *Le Pâtissier Glacier* and later *Memorial de la Pâtisserie*.

The paste used has been given various names:

1 *Pastillage:* Originated from the word *pastilles*, a type of lozenge sweet.
2 *Gum paste:* Icing sugar and starch mixed with moisture and gelatine.
3 *Gum dragon:* Made from the gum exuded by the dragon tree (*Astragulas*).
4 *Gum tragacanth:* Paste made from tragacanth, a binding agent.

TRAGACANTH

Also known as gum dragon, tragacanth is a gum exuded by several species of *Astragulas*, particularly *Astragulas Gummifer*. Originally known as Persian tragacanth, the tree flourishes in eastern countries and the Asian deserts. Tragacanth is mainly used as a vehicle for drugs, and as a binding agent for lozenges and pastilles. Various grades are available. Good quality tragacanth is white, tasteless, odourless and insoluble in alcohol; it can be purchased in powder and flake form. Although insoluble, tragacanth will absorb 15–20 times its own weight of water to give a thick gel.

GELATINE

Most gelatine is produced from the tissues of animal bones. It swells when soaked in cold water and dissolves, on boiling, to a viscid liquid, which solidifies to a jelly on cooling. Gelatine can be purchased in three forms: sheet, flake and powder. Gelatine should always be added to water and soaked sufficiently to obtain maximum swelling. Avoid prolonged soaking, however, which tends to destroy the gel strength. High temperature or prolonged heating also reduces the gel strength, and for most purposes gelatine solutions should not be heated above 60°C.

GUM ACACIA OR ARABIC

This product owes its name to the fact that it is the dried form of the gum exuded by a species of acacia – a tree which grows in East and West Africa, but was first known and used in Arabia. It has a faint odour and an insipid taste. It dissolves slowly in about twice its weight of water, forming a thick, transparent mucilage with an acid reaction. It is slightly soluble in dilute alcohol, but quite insoluble in liquids with more than 60 per cent alcohol. Warm water will give a better result and the solution should always be strained through a muslin before use.

Gum arabic is used in confectionery as a sealing agent, emulsifying agent, and as a binding agent in some types of paste work. It can be used as a thickening agent in colours for printing or painting on plaques made from royal icing or pastillage.

As a binding agent for sticking pieces of icing or pastillage together:

Ingredients	
Gum arabic	10 g
Water	20 g
Alcohol	5 g

Dissolve the gum in hot (not boiling) water and add the alcohol. Cool, store in a sealed container, and use as required.

As a shine for brushing over leaves, or any pastillage surface requiring a wet look:

Ingredients	
Gum arabic	20 g
Water	20 g

Dissolve the gum in the hot water and brush over the surfaces while warm. Re-heat gently if necessary.

■ PREPARING PASTILLAGE

Equipment
Sieve
Palette knife
Metal scraper
Paint brush
Bowl for gelatine or gum
Bowl for cornflour
Rolling pin
Large knife
Polythene bag
Ruler
Cutters
Modelling tools
Drying board

Prepare the necessary equipment and ingredients, ensuring all surfaces and utensils are clean. It helps to assemble all the utensils required, including a container with icing sugar and one of cornflour for dusting purposes.

BASIC RECIPE 1 (USING TRAGACANTH)

Ingredients	
Icing sugar	500 g
Cornflour	50 g
Water	40 ml
Tragacanth powder	30 g
Royal icing	25 g
Blue colouring	

Soak the gum in the cold water for about 18 hours, using a clean and covered container. Store in the refrigerator, as during warm weather it tends to deteriorate quickly. When soft and jelly-like in consistency, pass through clean muslin. Two or three drops of blue colouring can be added at this stage if the paste is to be kept white – the blue will enhance the whiteness.

Add the sieved icing sugar and cornflour in stages, mixing continuously to a smooth, pliable paste. Work in the royal icing and mix to a smooth, malleable paste – it should not be at all sticky. Store the paste in a double-thickness polythene bag, until required.

BASIC RECIPE 2 (USING GELATINE)

Ingredients	
Icing sugar	500 g
Cornflour	50 g
Water	40 ml
Leaf gelatine	10 g
Royal icing	25 g
Blue colouring	

Soak the gelatine in cold water. Sieve the icing sugar and cornflour onto a clean surface and make a large hollow (it is not advisable to use a marble slab for making the pastillage, as the coldness of the slab will cool the gelatine too quickly, causing lumps of re-setting gelatine to appear in the completed paste). Drain the gelatine thoroughly, place in a small saucepan, add the water and colouring (if used) and warm gently over low heat to dissolve. Pour the gelatine into the hollow, carefully draw in the icing sugar and mix to a smooth paste Continue as in method 1.

Preparing pastillage (basic recipe 2)

Work in the royal icing

Make a hollow in the icing sugar and cornflour and pour in the gelatine

Mould into a ball

Draw in the sugar and mix to a smooth paste

Either method used will give satisfactory results, although by using tragacanth the finished surface of the pastillage will look better. It is thus well worth acquiring the gum, which would be helpful in producing exhibition-standard work.

For occasional or speedy production of the paste, the gelatine method is preferred and the result can be extremely good, as the paste is ready to roll out immediately. It also has a malleable, elastic texture, making the rolling technique easy to carry out.

Points to note

1 To ensure whiteness, the slab and mixer's hands must be scrupulously clean.
2 Only use liquid colours, as paste-type colours can spoil the elasticity of the paste.
3 Colour added to the completed paste can result in an uneven or streaky look.
4 Speed in production of the paste is important, as the paste dries quickly.
5 If the paste tends to dry and crack while rolling, add a little royal icing.
6 If the paste is too wet, just add more icing sugar until it is smooth, pliable and not sticking to the surface.
7 Keep all scrapings from the table or hands separate; if the paste has lumps or an uneven texture it can spoil the finished surface of the rolled item.
8 Only use the amount required, and always store the remaining paste and trimmings in a separate polythene bag, in a well wrapped package.
9 Examine the condition of surfaces, prepared stencils and hands, as grease or dirty finger marks will permanently mark the surface of the pastillage.

Rolling the pastillage

Prepare the stencils and assemble all the necessary utensils, including a board or sheet of thick glass, evenly dusted with cornflour for storing the cut pieces.

Roll the pastillage to the desired thickness, occasionally rolling the sheet over the pin and dusting the surface with cornflour: do not be too generous with the cornflour, it will cause the pastillage to dry faster than necessary.

Test the thickness by cutting off a piece, but make sure that the centre of the sheet being rolled always remains thicker than the border. Before cutting, lightly dust the surface with cornflour and rub all over, using the palm of the hand. Massaging the surface for a few moments will produce the smooth, even surface desired in pastillage work. Do not leave the work at this stage, even for a minute; start cutting the planned pattern immediately.

Rolling the pastillage   The paste is rolled out to the thickness required, depending on the overall size, which means that for a large item a thicker paste will be required. Pastillage dries very quickly – if it is rolled out too thick, say 6 mm, it will initially be satisfactory in appearance, but eventually the centre will begin to dry, causing the rolled item to curl and buckle at the corners or edges. Therefore, apart from stocky pieces required for support purposes, no rolled pastillage should exceed 3 mm in thickness.

Uses

Rolled pastillage: Buildings, furniture, ornamental shapes, cards, and plaques.

Shaped pastillage: Trees, flowers, leaves, vegetables.

Moulded pastillage: Figures, boats, cars, wedding cake tops, etc.

With patience, perseverance and good organisation anything can be produced from pastillage. Advance preparation is vitally important, for example the stencils must be prepared and cut to the correct size. Some artistic flair is required in producing centrepieces from pastillage. Painting, drawing and sketching of some of the items will be necessary, but the only qualifications required for this are a desire and willingness to try and perhaps, as mentioned previously, a little patience.

An example of pastillage work

place another board of the same size on top, then turn over. Repeat the process until the pieces are completely dry on both sides. The pastillage pieces at this stage are extremely fragile; if damaged, the whole process will have to be repeated.

COMPLETING THE CUT PIECES

Gently brush the pieces with a soft paint brush, or rub a ball of cotton wool or a soft sponge all over, to eradicate any surplus corn-flour. Delicately rub the edges using fine sand-paper, but do not touch the surface area as it will spoil the smoothness. The surface can be improved by rubbing with a soft sponge dampened with hot water, using a fast circular motion; this will help in obtaining a smooth, shiny surface.

Cutting pastillage

Roll out the pastillage to the desired thickness

Cutting pastillage

Lay the stencil or ruler on top of the pastillage and cut along the edge; do not use pressure, but keep it in the correct position, wiping the knife on a damp cloth before and after cutting. Start cutting round the outside of the rolled pastillage and work towards the middle. When cutting, do not score with the knife, as it will wrinkle the edges. Place the cut pieces on the prepared board or glass to dry.

Depending on the size of the cut pieces, turn over after two hours (large pieces may need turning more frequently). For best results

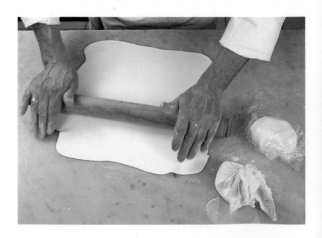

Cut out the pieces using stencils

Pastillage church

ASSEMBLING THE CUT PIECES

Have the presentation board or dish prepared and construct the pastillage object on it, so as not to have to move it later. Make sure you know the correct dimensions, to correctly marry up the different angles and shapes. Some support may be required initially; use a small paper cornet filled with royal icing to pipe along the edges being joined. Join the pieces together and run a soft paint brush over the joint to clear any surplus icing. Avoid excess icing, as it would be unnecessary and cause difficulties in keeping the joints tidy.

Allow to set completely. Continue the construction step by step, allowing each joint to dry completely before adding the next piece. Fill cracks or uneven places with icing, and gently rub over with a fine sandpaper, if necessary. Finish the centrepiece with piped decoration, using a paper cornet.

Templates for pastillage work

Precise cutting and constructing of pastillage designs can only be achieved with the help of a template. As mentioned previously, pastillage will loose its malleability if left for any length of time, so it is important to prepare the templates in advance. Once the template is cut for any specific item, it should be safely stored so that it can be re-used. Use a suitable material for the template.

Stencil card: Available in most art shops, easy to cut and waterproof.

Plastic/acetate: An easy to cut plastic would suffice, folder sleeves are ideal.

Metal: A thin and rigid metal would be adequate, but may be difficult to obtain.

Card: The most economical medium – any plain card without print is suitable.

Draw the geometrically accurate design on the stencil before cutting. Always leave a hanging edge on one side of the template, which will facilitate removing it when the cutting is completed.

Take care not to damage the template while cutting the pastillage; do not allow it to get wet, and always store it in a folder or envelope in a flat position. Prepare the template first on thin paper. The lines have to be cut with precision – for ease use a craft knife. Holding the template firmly on the rolled pastillage, produce clean cuts as close as possible to the line of the template. Scissors should not be used for cutting, as they will never give a precise cutting edge.

■ SHAPING OR MODELLING OF PASTILLAGE

Working with gum paste or pastillage gives any adventurous confectioner a large choice of items which can be produced. The paste can be shaped into various items: trees, leaves, vegetables, woven baskets and flowers. The completed items are used either for decorating cakes or as free-standing ornaments.

The pastillage needs to be malleable, as most of the work has to be done by hand, rather than using the rolling pin. As previously noted, pastillage dries very quickly once exposed, so it helps to add 20 g of liquid glucose to the basic recipe, and 10 g of soft white fat for the production of flowers. These ingredients will add moisture to the basic recipe and will slow the hardening of the pastillage. Alternatively, mixing one-third commercial sugar paste into the pastillage will result in a pliable paste, although this will not be suitable for items such as baskets or for making branches of trees and leaves.

The modelling paste is allowed to set in the refrigerator for about an hour, well wrapped or in a sealed container. It can be stored in a sealed container in the freezer, until required for further use. Leftover pieces of paste can be used by mixing in an equal quantity of freshly made paste just before using.

Use liquid colours if possible. If paste colour is a necessity, be careful with the amount of glycerol and glucose it contains: if used in excess, it can alter the texture and decrease the elasticity of the paste.

Casting or moulding of pastillage

Modelling by casting pastillage work is an art which is often considered a skill of the past – cake decoration items can now be readily bought made from plastic, paper, etc.

However, for an enthusiastic confectioner, the casting or moulding of pastillage should still occupy a considerable amount of time in study and practice. The basic pastillage recipe can be used satisfactorily for most designs; if a softer texture is required for very small items, the modelling paste with glucose can also work quite well. This will take longer to set, allowing time to shape or sculpt the items as required. Using the tip of a modelling knife and tools, minute details and features can be distinctively produced. If necessary, rub fine sandpaper gently over the surface of the item when completely dry, to give a smooth, fine texture.

Moulds are required for this type of work. They can be prepared by the confectioner, using plaster of Paris, from figures modelled with plasticine or wax. Metal moulds, such as Easter egg moulds, are also suitable.

TO PRODUCE CASTING MOULDS
Moulds for casting sugarcraft material are available commercially but, obviously, they may not suit individual requirements, in size or shape. You can also make your own moulds to suit any requirement.

To produce a doll mould, first make a wooden frame double the size of the required figure. Line the inside with tinfoil and half-fill with soft plaster. Generously brush the face or body of a plastic doll with icing sugar and press this halfway into the soft plaster. Make an incision, using a small knife, on each side from the object to the frame – this is to allow air to travel through, and for a tool to be inserted for removing the pastillage. When the plaster has set – test by rubbing a finger on the surface: it should not mark it – prepare a second batch of soft plaster and pour over the object, filling to approximately 2–3 mm above the top. Allow to set completely. Using a palette knife, pull apart the two halves. Remove the object and the mould is ready for the pastillage, marzipan, etc.

Using similar techniques, various suitable objects can be used for producing moulds for casting: fresh fruits, ceramic items, cupids, animals or spheres, etc.

CASTING TECHNIQUES

For casting or moulding, the pastillage must be pliable and soft, but not sticky. The inside of the moulds can be dusted using a muslin bag filled with cornflour, tapped gently over the mould. The pastillage is then rolled out to the length and thickness required. Avoid using excessive paste or rolling it out too far, as this will cause difficulties in the operation.

Without hesitating, lay the rolled paste over the mould and gently press it into the dusted mould, using the tip of the fingers or a small piece of sponge or cotton wool. Creases may form while inserting the paste into the mould. This can be avoided by gently rubbing the paste inside the mould, as it is being pressed in. Too much pressure must not be used or the paste is likely to stick. Using a sharp, damp knife, cut off the surplus paste level with the edge of the mould. A slight tap of the edge of the mould on the table, with a cloth in between, should be sufficient to relieve the casting.

If support is required, the mould can be strengthened by fixing a fine netting at the back or inside. This is done by brushing the mould with a thick solution of gum arabic and laying the net on top. When dry, tap gently on the edge of the mould, then remove the set pastillage by inserting a small knife in the incision and lifting gently. Complete as required, removing any surplus sugar and smoothing the surface with the aid of small piece of damp sponge.

■ COLOURING PASTILLAGE

Pastillage items can be successfully coloured by adding colours to the liquid when producing the mix. If deep colours are used it is essential to allow the gum paste to stand, well wrapped, until the colour develops. If the desired shade is not achieved more can then be added, but if excessive colour is used, the texture will be altered and the paste may not then be as pliable or elastic as expected.

Use as much paste as will be needed to complete all the intended items in one particular colour. It is better to prepare a little more than necessary, as it is virtually impossible to repeat shades and tints. Experimenting by mixing different shades can produce very effective results.

To obtain three shades from the same colour:
1   Starting off with a white batch, divide the gum paste in two equal parts. Colour one part to form the darkest required shade.
2   Divide the dark-coloured gum paste in two. Add half of this to half of the white paste to make a lighter shade.
3   Divide this batch again and mix with the remaining white, resulting in a very light shade.

The shades can be adjusted, adding more white paste as required. Keep all portions of pastes well wrapped during the operation.

Avoid exposing deep-shaded pastillage to bright sunlight as this will fade the colours very quickly.

Balance of colours: Some colours give the feeling of warmth while others seem cool. The reason for this is scientific but also psychological, as we associate colours with things like fire or the sea. Look again at the colour wheel (page 7): the reds and oranges on the left side are warm while the greens and blues on the right are cool. Also notice how each colour has varying degrees of warmth or coolness; some blues contain a lot of green and are therefore cooler than the ones which contain some red. In pastillage displays, colours can often be better identified by constructing a three-dimensional effect, which will distinguish the colours prominently. This technique is important for exhibition-type work.

Painting on pastillage

Painting on sugar is generally used to write a message on seasonal or celebration cakes, or to create scenes, figures or flowers. Remember that eating certain colours may not be appealing to the palate – although food colourings are classified as edible, fundamentally they are not. However, painting on sugarcraft work, such as plaques, or pastillage *pièces montées* for exhibition entries, is necessary and requires practice, patience, flair and creativity.

Pastillage is absorbent, and this has a bearing on the quality and texture of food colouring used. Always use clean, smooth, good-quality artist's brushes, in a range of different sizes. Experimenting with various mediums on discarded pieces of pastillage can help obtain the correct texture. For example,

colour pastes which contain glycerine and glucose will not dry. Liquid colours will often run, spread or bleed. The best results are obtained using the colour in powder form, moistened with a little water, glycerine and gum arabic. This will give excellent paste colour, and if applied on drawn designs can produce authentic shades.

Sketching and drawing

SKETCHING

It is an essential skill to be able to sketch on a sugar surface as on paper. Being creative in sugarcraft, particularly when sketching on pastillage, means being able to create a pattern of figures, flowers, buildings, animals and various characters.

The prepared and dried pastillage piece, whether in the form of a plaque, shield or the face of a building, requires some preparation.

Always begin the sketching or drawing with a clean, tidy surface. Sit at the table at a comfortable height, in a good light, and place a card on the surface to rest your hand on while working.

Always place the piece on a soft surface to do the sketching – a sponge, soft cloth or a layer of tissues would be adequate. If you sketch on a firm surface the pastillage could easily break.

Having decided on the subject to be sketched, keep a similar illustration beside you as a guide. It may help to do the sketch on paper first; this will give you confidence for the pastillage artwork. Using a very fine pointed pencil, mark the pastillage very lightly, particularly if the piece is to be painted. Sketching and drawing is only recommended for non-edible items – those which are removable or used purely for the purpose of display or exhibiting. Lead pencil markings should not be seen on the completed pastillage work.

TRACING

Sketch the design on waxed paper, then reverse the paper and place on the pastillage. Rub lightly with the tip of a biro which will transfer the design on the pastillage. The technique is sometimes fiddly, as it is difficult to keep the paper firm and accurately in position.

DRAWING

Learning to draw is largely a matter of practice and observation. Be self-critical, practise on paper, and if it looks wrong start again. The fourth attempt will often look better than the first; do not re-trace the lines.

Follow the same basic principles as for sketching and avoid leaving fingermarks on the surface of the pastillage, as these cannot be deleted. To capture the character of the subject you are drawing, be inventive with your drawing technique. For example, when drawing a leaf, the different textures can be achieved by using short, sharp strokes. Geometric knowledge is also essential to ensure that the drawing is in perspective. The confectioner will require a sharp hard pencil, set-square, compass and ruler.

TYPES OF LINES

Drawing can be executed in various types of lines, depending entirely on the work to be done.

1 *Wire line:*   A clean line for sharp drawing.
2 *Calligraphic line:*   Characterised by various widths, ideal for lettering.
3 *Broken line:*   Repeated at points, ideal for figures and flowers.
4 *Repeated lines:*   Loose and parallel lines, freer outlines, for sketching.

Drawing lines on larger pieces of pastillage should be done before the pieces are assembled. Make sure they are dry, and always place the piece on a soft surface. *Do not place any pressure on the pastillage while drawing.*

Wood grain and marble effect

This technique can be mastered successfully by practising with two or three shades; experimenting is essential. Speed of production is also important, as pastillage will harden on the surface quickly if left just for a moment. Cracks will then be formed when rolled, more prominent when using deep-coloured pastes, and the skin will break, giving the surface a 'stretch-mark' effect, obviously not suitable if the aim is to obtain a smooth and even surface.

It is a good idea to have a large sheet of thin plastic at hand, to keep the rolled paste covered from one step to the next.

Prepare three or four shades of pastillage, following the colouring instructions previously described (page 83). Make sure you colour sufficient paste to complete the whole project from the same rolled-out batch: it would be practically impossible to obtain the same shade from a second batch. Trimmings are not suitable for re-rolling.

Equipment
Rolling pin
Knife
Palette knife
Ruler
Templates
Damp cloth
Drying board or glass
Bowl for cornflour

WOOD GRAIN PATTERN

Ensure the working surface is clean and dry and prepare the stencils.

1 Using the damp cloth, dampen the working surface.
2 Roll each shade of pastillage to a sausage shape, about 20 cm in length.
3 Join four rolled pieces together.
4 Fold the pastillage over, producing a large sausage shape.
5 Roll out to about 20 cm in length, keeping the colours together; avoid twisting or spiralling.
6 Cut into three equal lengths, join together and repeat this process three or four times, keeping the coloured paste in straight lines.
7 Fold the pastillage into four, keeping it flat on the surface.
8 Start rolling out the pastillage, stretching the paste lengthways first, then widening until the correct thickness is attained.
9 Keep the rolled piece covered with plastic to prevent a skin forming.
10 Using the prepared template and a damp knife, cut along the edges and complete the centrepieces as desired.

Note: If knots are wanted in the pattern, form the rolled sausage shape into a spiral shape, then roll as previously described.

Producing a wood-grain effect

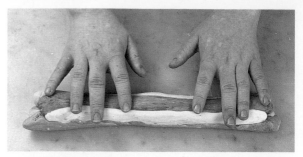

Roll into a sausage shape

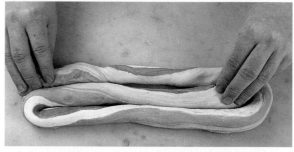

Fold the sausage as shown and repeat the process

Roll into a spiral

Join the pastillage strips together

Roll out the pastillage to the desired thickness

Pastillage tray

MARBLE EFFECT

Prepare and colour the pastillage as for the wood grain technique. A successful marbled effect can be achieved by using just two colours, 50% of each. Divide the colours in various small pieces and roll into balls. Mingle them together, dispersing the shades, and very lightly mix together. Roll out as for the grain technique.

■ PASTILLAGE PLATE

Equipment
Polythene bag for pastillage
Bowl for cornflour
Rolling pin
Knife
Crimpers
Soft sponge
Sandpaper
Paper cornet and piping tube

Once you have decided on the plate to be used as the mould, dust the surface lightly with cornflour. Use a muslin pouch filled with cornflour and powder the plate by shaking the muslin pad against your hand.

Prepare the pastillage, colour as necessary and roll out thinly to 2 mm, just sufficient to cover the plate and hang slightly over the edge. Using a clean, damp knife, cut all round

Wood-grain pastillage plate

the edge of the plate using a sawing movement. Gently rub your finger along the cut edge, to eliminate any remaining crumbs of pastillage. Tap the plate gently over a surface to ease the rolled paste on the plate: you must make sure the pastillage is not stuck to the plate at this stage, otherwise it will stick when dry.

If crimping is desired, it should be done immediately. Use the crimper by placing an elastic band on the handle, restricting the power of the opening; crimp round the plate, rotating the plate continuously so the pattern is uniform and accurately spaced out.

Using a soft brush, clean the surface to eliminate any sugar dust. Allow to dry for at least 8–10 hours. When dry, gently remove the dry pastillage from the plate, turn over, and store in a safe place to dry the other side. The pastillage plate can be completed in various decorative ways, using a paper cornet and number 0 or 1 icing tube. Allow to dry.

The centre of the plate can be decorated with a spray of flowers, or filled with petits fours for the purpose of display.

■ PASTILLAGE CASKET

Equipment
Bowl for cornflour
Rolling pin
Knife
Ruler
Template
Board or glass for drying

Prepare the template, cut accurately and in the correct dimensions, and colour the pastillage

Pastillage casket

as required. Roll the pastillage on a lightly dusted surface to about 1–2 mm thick, depending on the size of the casket. Place the template on the rolled paste and, holding it delicately in position, cut using a clean, damp knife; avoid using a scoring movement as this will cause ridged edges. With the aid of a palette knife, place the cut pieces on a lightly dusted board or piece of glass and allow to dry for about two hours. Then gently turn the pieces over to dry the other side for another two hours, or until well dry. If the pieces are allowed to stay at the semi-dry stage for a long period, they will curl at the corners and the shape will buckle. If large, they will probably need to be turned over again and allowed to dry for a further period.

Assembling the casket

Some sort of support is required while the pieces bond together. Pipe a small amount of royal icing on the edges to be attached, join them together, and allow this to dry thoroughly before joining on the next piece. Do not disturb the piece, as a slight movement can upset the position of the pieces, and eventually the dimensions of the centrepiece will be permanently distorted. Always store the drying pieces, while working and at completion, in a safe, clean place, away from the kitchen working environment (i.e. away from excessive heat, steam and direct sunlight). Decorate the completed casket in an attractive, decorative fashion, using a paper cornet and number 1 or 2 icing tube. The aerograph has become a useful piece of equipment; a little shading before piping would enhance the appearance of the casket. The completed casket can be filled with flowers or chocolates, used for presenting petits fours, or as a decorative centrepiece.

■ PASTILLAGE FLOWERS

Many books are available which specialise in making flowers using sugar paste, and each of the authors will probably have their own special recipe for making the paste, in most cases all contain either tragacanth or gelatine as the setting ingredient in the sugar. Pastillage can be made more adaptable by incorporating glucose and a small amount of white fat, which will produce a smooth, malleable texture. Also, mixing one-third commercial sugar paste to one batch of pastillage will produce a very effective paste for making sugar flowers. To achieve perfection, you should ideally have a real flower to study the shape and colour.

Regardless of the flower you intend to produce, always begin with a small rolled-up ball, then immediately shape into the flower.

HAND MOULDING A ROSE PETAL
Colour the paste as desired, then create a shape using the fingers and the palm of the hand. Manipulating a lump of paste into a petal is a technique that has to be mastered – practice and experience will help you make a correct flower.

Pull out a small amount of paste, the size of a walnut; the petal will determine the size of the rose. To be effective the rose petals must be thin; dip your fingers in a little cornflour and massage the paste until it is thin and almost transparent. Each petal produced is immediately attached to form the shape of rose, brushing the base of each petal with egg white or a thick solution of gum arabic.

1 Fold the top of the petal into a point to resemble a bud and place to one side.
2 Produce a second petal, again with a thin texture, and immediately attach to the base of the bud.
3 Repeat the process, attaching three petals

round the base, each one slightly over-lapping each other, with the top thin edges lightly curling outwards. At this stage it could serve as a rose bud.

4   Produce another petal, a little larger than the previous three; placing the petal in the palm of the hand, lightly rub with your finger to produce a concave shape.

5   Lightly pinch the top edge, curling it out-wards, and gently make an indentation with the fingers to form a slight downward curve in the classic shape of the rose petal.

6   Attach to the base of the bud.

7   Produce two more petals, resulting in a rose with 6 petals in all, excluding the centre.

8   The rose could be complete at this stage, or further petals can be added to make the rose larger.

VARIEGATED MARKING ON PETALS

To produce a fine coloured edge on each petal, simply add a very tiny rolled piece of model-ling paste in a darker shade round the initial ball. Roll into a ball again and form the petal as previously described, making sure the darker colour remains on the edge; on stretching the paste, it will be found the darker shade will get much thinner. The coloured rim on the flowers will look very attractive and enhance the presentation.

WIRING THE ROSE

The size of the rose will obviously determine its weight; to support the flower upright, a 22 gauge florist's wire would suffice. Form a hook at the end of the wire, dip into egg white and shape a small cone at the end of the wire; allow to set. Add the petals as previously described round the cone, which should not be seen when the rose is complete. Stand the wire in a bottle while the flower is being produced, to avoid damaging the soft petals.

CALYX

Roll out some dark green modelling paste, then using a small knife, cut five small pointed leaves. Dampen the bases with a little egg white and attach them round the base under the rose; curl the points outward.

MAKING ROSE LEAVES

Colour the modelling paste dark green, then roll it out thinly (1 mm). Using a small, point-ed knife, cut an elongated shape ending in a point; mark the veins of the leaf. Attach a fine florist's wire (26 gauge) dipped in egg white, pinching the base of the leaf. Allow to set, with the leaf slightly curved to create a natural shape. Improve the green by shading the leaf using green dusting powder. Leaf cutters and vein marking moulds are available to give a realistic leaf appearance. Combine five wired leaves to form a spray of leaves, using floristry tape to bind the wires together.

4 MARZIPAN

■ INTRODUCTION

Marzipan is used extensively in the pastry and confectionery trades as a covering for celebration cakes, as petits fours, as a modelling medium and as an ingredient for fancies or tortes. It is also used as a stuffing for dates, and sandwiched between nuts for dipping. The marzipan or almond paste can vary in quality and cost – some cheaper covering pastes are made from a blend of ground peanuts and almonds but cannot be called marzipan. Commercial products such as Battenburg, French fancies, marzipan fruits and figures use real marzipan (almond paste) or covering paste depending on the sale price of the goods. Some bakers and confectioners still make their own marzipan; care needs to be taken to age or rest the paste before being used for celebration cakes, otherwise oil will stain the royal icing and look unpleasant.

A selection of almonds and pastes

■ ALMONDS

Almonds are the fruit of the almond tree. They vary in quality, the best types being those called Jordan, Valencia, Malaga, Palma and Gorganti. Smaller varieties are the Sicilian and Bari almonds, with the Jaffi and Barber almond being of a lesser quality. The major import of almonds comes from Italy and Spain. The almond is rich in oil. Sweet almond oil has no flavour and can be produced from both sweet and bitter almonds. Essential or bitter almond oil is extracted from bitter almonds which are crushed and blended with water. Here the enzyme emulsin reacts with the amygdalin present to produce benzaldehyde, dextrose and prussic acid. Benzaldehyde is freed from the poisonous prussic acid and is used as essence of almond. Cheaper coal-tar-based toluene is used for almond flavourings.

Cropping the almonds

The largest of the almond types are those from Spain, giving approximately 16 almonds to 1 oz or 28 g. Small almonds give approximately 45 to the 1 oz or 28 g. Almonds are divided into two types: hard shell or soft shell nuts. Europe tends to produce the hard shell type of almond, with California producing mainly the soft shelled varieties.

The almond tree takes up to seven years to bear fruit and about 5–7 years to reach maturity. Older trees will cease to bear fruit and are replaced. The crop tends to be bi-annual, i.e. a heavy crop one year will result in a much lighter crop the following season. Growers say that a tree bearing an abundance of fruit will produce small almonds, whereas a tree bearing a small crop will produce large

An almond tree

almonds. It will require approximately 1.5 kg of unshelled nuts to produce 500 g of almond kernels.

Processing

First the almonds are weighed and graded according to size; any foreign material, dust or shell, is removed. Next, during storage, the nuts are sprayed to kill any traces of moth, weevil or insect. Blanching follows, and here the outer skin is removed to reveal the white surface of the nut kernel. The almonds are then washed and transferred to picking tables where they are checked and any other foreign matter is removed.

The nut is either left whole or made into shapes by cutting to form strip, split, nibbed, flaked and, finally, ground almonds.

Granite rollers are used to grind the almond in the production of marzipan and cooling takes place under careful conditions to prevent oil separation. Almond oil, which is also produced as part of the blanching process from the residue almond matter, is used widely by the cosmetics industry.

■ PREPARATION OF MARZIPAN

Most marzipan, almond and covering pastes are purchased from wholesalers or large manufacturers. The paste must be kept covered and cool when not in use, away from any strong-smelling foods or materials. Remove the required quantity of paste and mould, dusting with icing sugar to make the paste pliable. In cold weather this can be difficult – break the paste into smaller pieces and mix slowly for a few minutes on a mixing machine with the dough hook attachment. If the paste is over-handled or mixed, the oil content will surface and cause problems for handling,

especially if used for wedding or birthday cakes. When using marzipan on a cake, leave it to stand after covering to dry for 48 hours.

When rolling out marzipan, use a marble slab or clean stainless steel work top – never use wood. The recipes provided on pages 94 and 95 all make a useful paste which should be made well in advance of use to avoid oiling problems.

Commercial and retail sales

Commercial units of marzipan can be purchased in 2.5, 5 and 10 kg, whereas the retail sector generally uses 250 or 500 g packs. The cost of these products is high because of the almond content; pastes using a different nut content tend to be cheaper but do not have the distinctive flavour or characteristics of real marzipan. The paste will be wrapped and sealed to prevent it from drying and becoming hard. Always feel the edges of the pack to check for hardness: the paste should press leaving an indent; old or dry paste will have a tough edge or surface and should not be used.

Marzipan regulations and ingredients

Marzipan is a blend of sugar and freshly blanched almonds ground together in a melangeur or between rollers until very smooth. During this process the mix is heated and when finished it is a smooth, plastic, homogeneous paste.

A code of practice was initiated in 1969 to cover marzipan, almond paste and almond icing. The terms of this code are as follows:

1   For the purposes of this code the word 'marzipan' wherever it occurs is to be read as if it referred also to almond paste and almond icing.

The word 'sell' includes offer or expose for sale or have in possession for sale; and 'sold' shall be construed accordingly.

2 Marzipan sold as such shall contain not less than 23.5% of dry almond substance and no other nut ingredient. Not less than 75% of the remainder shall be solid carbohydrate sweetening matter.

3 Any food sold under such a description as to lead an intending purchaser to believe he is purchasing marzipan, or sold in response to a request for marzipan, shall comply with the standard of composition in paragraph 2.

4 This code shall not apply to:
   i   articles such as cake decorations, figures and petits fours;
   ii single articles of sugar confectionery, weighing less than 3 oz/85 g;
   iii any article weighing less than 1 oz/28 g in a composite chocolate and/or confectionery assortment;
   iv bars or blocks coated with chocolate and/or sugar confectionery, which have a declared net weight not exceeding 4 oz/112 g.

5 If flour confectionery is sold with a claim that it is covered partly or wholly with, or contains, marzipan, then the marzipan shall comply with the standard of composition in paragraph 2.

Marzipan and almond paste recipes

Confusion exists over the terms marzipan and almond paste. Raw marzipan is made up of two parts blanched almonds and one part sugar. Almond paste, however, is made up of one part almonds and two parts sugar, together with sufficient egg or glucose to make a pliable paste.

FRENCH MARZIPAN

Ingredients	
Blanched almonds	1 kg
Bitter almonds	28.35 g
Sugar	1.5 kg
Water	450 ml
Glucose	75 g

Blanch and shred the almonds. Boil the water, glucose and sugar to 117.5°C. Mix with the almonds and cool. Grind the mixture to a fine paste. Wrap the paste well and store.

GERMAN MARZIPAN

Ingredients	
Blanched almonds	1 kg
Bitter almonds	28.35 g
Icing sugar	750 g
Granulated sugar	850 g

Blanch and shred the almonds. Grind them coarsely with the granulated sugar. Dry the mixture in a pan over a solid-top stove. Cool and grind the mixture with the icing sugar.

MARZIPAN

Ingredients	
Ground almonds	2 kg
Sugar	5 kg
Glucose	250 g
Rosewater	28 ml

Boil the sugar and water to a soft ball at 115°C. Add the ground almonds and mix well. Cool and mould the mixture, dusting with icing sugar. Wrap and store until required.

ALMOND PASTE

Ingredients	
Ground almonds	453 g
Caster sugar	453 g
Icing sugar	453 g
Egg yolk	175 g
Orange flower water	56 ml

Mix all the ingredients to a pliable paste. Wrap the paste well in a plastic bag and seal. Store and use as required.

ALMOND PASTE – BOILED

Ingredients	
Ground almonds	453 g
Caster sugar	906 g
Water	285 ml
Orange flower water	56 ml
Glucose	56 g

Boil the water and sugar to 115°C. Stir in the glucose and flower water. Add the ground almonds and mix well. Cool the paste, wrap well and store.

Marzipan and almond paste can also be made from hazelnuts, walnuts and pistachio nuts; chocolate, coffee and apricot marzipan is used in Europe.

Hygiene, handling and storage

Marzipan and almond paste needs to be handled very carefully, as pastry and bakery environments provide ideal conditions for the growth of bacteria and mould. Marzipan is liable to ferment if flour is in contact with the paste. Yeast spores will contaminate and ferment the paste, causing the product, such as a celebration cake, to bulge and develop a strong alcohol flavour. When working marzipan you should be extremely clean and organised. Dampness affects marzipan and almond-based goods; almond paste or marzipan coverings will sweat on the surface and are susceptible to mould growth if not kept in cool dry conditions.

Marzipan paste or products need to be stored correctly to preserve their shelf life. Keep the base paste well wrapped in a cool, dry, well-ventilated store. On no account keep marzipan in a humid atmosphere or one where flour is likely to come in contact. Wrap the paste first in two layers of clingfilm and then place in a thick plastic bag, remove as much air as possible and seal well. Almond paste or marzipan will keep for some months if kept in these conditions. If the air is allowed to get to the pastes then a crust will form and the product will not be usable.

Check the stock of paste to ensure no fermentation has occurred or the pastes are drying; check for mould growth or infestation of any kind. Do not mix pastes from different batches if possible, and use stock in rotation – first in then first out. Ensure the paste does not sweat during humid or close days as this can lead to mould growth. On no account use a paste where mould is evident: this needs to be discarded.

Wash all bowls and equipment well before commencing work and ensure your hands are meticulously clean at all times. Work away from the main production area, preferably in a cool room separate from the main area. Wrap all pastes at all times, except when required for the task. Wash your hands regularly – if a film of paste sticks to the hands it will attract dirt from trays and equipment.

Wash tools and cutters regularly to ensure clean fresh work is produced. I wrap my plastic tools and keep them frozen in a cool box when working with pastes for modelling – this keeps the oil from becoming a problem when producing fine work. Wear clean work wear; never use the same wear for making yeast goods then move to almond paste or marzipan production: the risk of fermentation is too high. Common sense should prevail; professional pâtissiers are hygienic in nature and prepare and organise themselves accordingly; poor hygiene leads to poor products and lack of business. Thankfully, there is a growing awareness where food hygiene is concerned, with a more professional attitude within the craft itself. Young people are keen to work in a safe and hygienic manner and we must all take responsibility for such education to promote higher standards.

MIXING

Marzipan can be mixed with colour and flavour for a range of confectionery and pastry goods. The most important rule to remember is that large quantities of paste which are coloured and/or flavoured need to be rested prior to use, or the almond oil can cause problems. Small quantities for decoration purposes can be used straightaway. Mix any paste in a stout mixing machine on slow speed; never mix on higher speeds as this might cause damage to the gearing system. Small quantities can be flavoured and coloured by hand, using either mixed flavour or colour compounds.

PACKAGING

When produced, paste is best stored wrapped in 2–3 layers of clingfilm and placed in a plastic bag with the air removed as far as is possible. Keep the paste in a cool, dry store and avoid any contact with cornflour or flour to prevent fermentation.

PROBLEMS

Old or poorly stored marzipan will become dry and crumble; in damp conditions mould can occur or the paste can ferment. Marzipan that is too hard or dry and crumbles may be softened with glucose or fondant, but usually this will still leave fine hard lumps; re-mix slowly and stand for 48 hours.

COLOURINGS AND FLAVOURINGS

Marzipan can be purchased white, yellow or in green and pink colours for production of small animals and fruits. The preferred colour is white, but this is expensive. Raw marzipan has a dull colour and is mixed with glucose and icing sugar to produce modelling marzipan paste. Yellow marzipan or covering pastes are used for cake coverings and Battenburg products, but the colouring is not as effective as with natural paste.

Colouring needs to be carried out with care: too much and the effect will not be pleasing to the eye; too little and the finish might be insipid. Use a powdered or paste-based colour; water-based colours require a lot to be added to achieve the necessary tint. Powdered cake colours produce excellent results when mixed with a little alcohol or just used dry. When modelling, make all the light colours first and then the darker colours last to avoid staining. Make up all coloured pastes before any production occurs; this again avoids smears and marks on finished goods. Flavouring can complement the colour: the list below gives a typical colour–flavour balance:

Yellow	lemon, banana, pineapple, pear or melon
Green	apple, mint, greengage, pear, lime or pistachio
Orange	orange, apricot, clementine or mango
Brown	chocolate or coffee
Pink	rose
Red	strawberry, raspberry or cherry
Purple	plum or grape

Colouring needs to meet with the Food and Drugs Act (The Colouring Matter in Food

Regulations 1973). Paste consistency is affected when liquid-based colours are used: use a powder colour dissolved in alcohol or a paste/glycerine-based colour.

■ MODELLING MARZIPAN

Recipes for modelling paste

The Renshaw recipes given below produce an excellent paste for model items, pièce montée work and fine intricate competition work.

MARZIPAN RECIPE I

Ingredients	
Renmarz raw marzipan or almond paste	2.75 kg
Icing sugar (bride cake sugar)	2 kg
Liquid glucose	500 g

Warm the glucose to 83°C and add to the marzipan, mixing on a slow speed in a machine using the dough hook. Add the icing sugar and mix to a smooth paste; colour as required.

MARZIPAN RECIPE 2

Ingredients	
Renmarz raw marzipan or almond paste	2.75 kg
Icing sugar (bride cake sugar)	2 kg
Liquid glucose	200 g
Invert sugar	200 g

MARZIPAN RECIPE 3

Ingredients	
Renmarz raw marzipan or almond paste	2.75 kg
Icing sugar (bride cake sugar)	2 kg
Liquid glucose	175 g
Invert sugar	285 g

Recipes 2 and 3 only need to be mixed to a smooth paste and not warmed as in recipe 1.

Modelling tools for marzipan work

To produce any marzipan work you will require some basic tools, these can be pur-

MODELLING EQUIPMENT

Ball tool	Brass and/or aluminium box rollers
Grooved spatula	Leaf moulds and cutters
Double-ended gouge	Sprung flower cutters
Plain double-ended spatula	Netal or plastic cutters, assorted
Double-ended cone tool	Artist's palette
Double-ended paddle, plain	Small stepped palette knife
Double-ended serrated paddle	Plastic scrapers, small and large
Selection of fine paint brushes	Piping tubes, assorted
Cocktail sticks	Aerograph spray gun
Small sharp knife	Compressed air canister
Selection of pastry crimpers	Powdered and paste colours
Flat nylon board	Small and large needle
Small sharp scissors	Small stainless steel bowl
Fine pastry brush	Small grater or sago board
Plastic rolling pin	Selection of sharp modelling knives

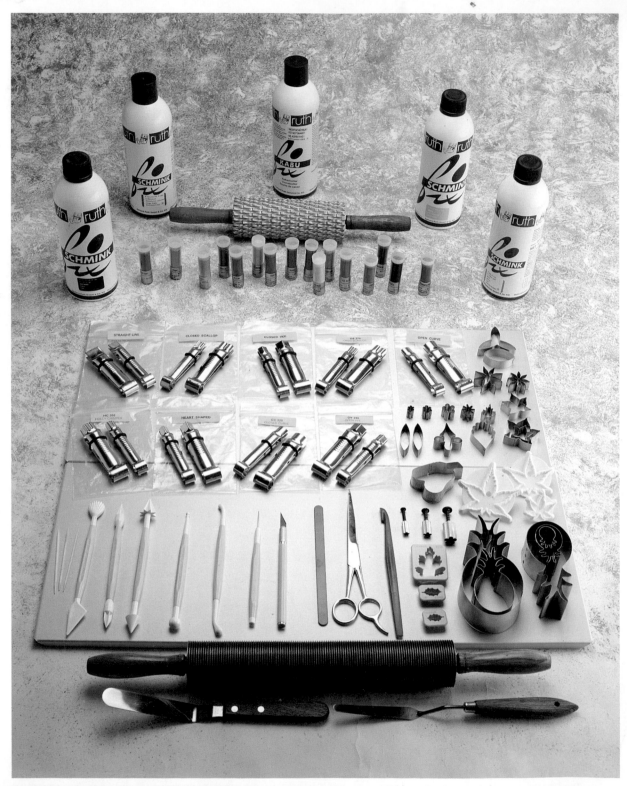

A selection of small tools needed for marzipan work

chased from cake artistry and kitchen centres or from specialist confectionery stockists.

BOX ROLLERS

Box rollers can be either plastic, aluminium or brass. The roller has an indented pattern which, when rolled over sheets of paste, leaves a decorative marking. These can be basket weave, grooved or pin-point designs. I prefer the heavier brass tools, but these are not so readily available. Box rollers are useful for covering surfaces with a different design than the usual flat surface and are ideal for pastillage modelling, marzipan or chocolate modelling pastes.

CUTTERS

Cutters enable difficult shapes and forms to be produced; buy high-quality cutters which will last if cared for. These can be very expensive and need to be kept secure; never lend your collection of cutters – others may not take the care and attention that you would. Metal and plastic cutters of all shapes and sizes can be collected from cake artistry suppliers or cake artistry centres.

Cutters should be kept in a strong tin to prevent them from being damaged or pressed out of shape. Do not store them, or any modelling tools, with everyday knives, or damage will occur.

TEMPLATES

Template shapes are useful as a guide when making cake decorations, centrepieces, gâteaux, tortes or novelty cakes. Crayon colouring books provide simple template shapes which can be photocopied and used to cut out a good template. Alternatively, make your own from thick card, sheet plastic or fine modelling plywood. Card templates can be used for almond wafer mixtures – spread over and baked, then formed into a shape while hot for desserts or hotel sweets.

Collect leaves in autumn, place them flat on a copier and produce a natural template; cut these from thin sheet plastic and use them time and again. The tops of multi-portion foil trays make excellent template material for quick production of wafer biscuit shapes.

ALMOND WAFER RECIPE FOR TEMPLATE DESIGNS

Ingredients	
Ground almonds	400 g
Icing sugar	600 g
Soft flour	200 g
Egg whites	200 g
Milk	200 ml

Sieve the dry ingredients. Add the milk and whites, blend carefully and allow the mixture to stand for 1 hour. Spread over the template with a palette knife and bake in a moderate oven (193–204°C). Remove from the oven and, while still hot, mould the wafer into the required shape. This will set almost immediately and therefore only a few templates should be baked at any one time. If the wafer sets, re-heat it in the oven and mould.

Modelling techniques

There is no one definitive technique for producing modelled marzipan work. Each person will develop their own technique and find out how best to produce a creative piece of art. Many of the fine artists working today have individual techniques which often are undisclosed. There are two types of artist: first, the person who can create quality work from inherent skills as a natural artist; second, the dedicated person determined to overcome the difficulty in creating original art work. The latter needs more time to develop a technique or skill which the natural artist often does without thinking: each stage will be dissected, studied and planned. Many people will identify with the latter. Everyone must develop their own techniques, through discussion with those who are more knowledgeable, sharing views and tips. Without such exchange a select few will always dominate and the future culture of the craft will diminish.

Advance preparation is important: planning, studying and drawing thumb sketches of the pieces to be produced. Practice and trial are the seeds of competence. Ask questions, analyse work scientifically, investigate and probe for those guarded tips.

When a certain shape is needed, play about with different tools – these may be knitting needles or other household items. Children's toys have often offered a guide for a particular shape when making bears or miniature insects, but by far the best results are achieved using your hands. Even the smallest items of a ladybird can be formed with your palm and one finger. Keep your hands scrupulously clean when working with marzipan. Wash your hands often – this cannot be stressed too much – keep your work bench tidy and wrap each colour of paste as it is used to prevent drying.

Polish marzipan with your fingers. If you have warm hands then modelling will be problematic. Work in a cool room, use clingfilm and plastic gloves to prevent a good surface being marked with fingerprints. Gently rubbing over a seam or join will gradually blend the paste into an even surface, especially where clothing on figure work is concerned. Plan a piece with a good balance of colour, shape, texture and height; work on small pieces first then build up to more complex scenes. Lightly wrap finished products with layers of clingfilm to protect individual figures.

Competition standards

To produce a piece suitable for entry in a competition, where your standard will be judged against others, your work needs to be high quality, artistic, able to create interest, and have a form and balance which will capture the judges' attention immediately. Select a novel theme; if you think yours is original then you are probably wrong: choose current comic themes from TV or cartoon characters.

Be unusual rather than formal, but remember, even the most basic animals, if worked to perfection, will capture an audience. Simple work of high quality will always be admired. Keep notes and pictures of other work, discuss these with the creator, learn from their mistakes and be prepared to invest a lot of time in your work.

When creating a competition piece for the first time, use reference pictures to assist in the relationships of size. Study any literature on art and form to understand how to proportion a piece in relation to others. If working with cartoon characters, for example, then you do have the freedom to create fun-type models where the relationship of form is not so critical.

■ NOVELTY FIGURES AND ANIMALS

Making a marzipan clown

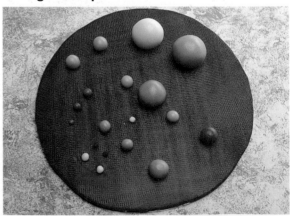

Prepare the different-coloured marzipans and portion into balls

Form the individual parts

Assemble the clown

Marzipan is used to make novelty figures for display and sale; these can be simple or more complex to produce. Using a few basic tools and a little time you can create interesting artistic, comical, cartoon or serious figures. Marzipan work has grown in this country over the past few years; in Europe many countries produce excellent daily fare in marzipan. Any figure must be fairly quick to produce for commercial purposes: the time involved and the cost of the marzipan would otherwise price the work out of the market. Keep your figures funny and simple. Colour the required amount of marzipan to produce each figure. If you are making a large quantity, prepare trays for storage of each stage as the figures are produced. Prepare and complete a batch at a time, but don't attempt to produce all the figures in one go or parts will dry and not bond together well.

The finished pieces benefit from being dried for a couple of hours to form a skin, and then the pieces are joined with chocolate. Some figure work is best joined when the paste is soft, but take care not to impress your finger prints in the marzipan. Plastic gloves of the surgical type can make handling more easy. Wash your hands often to prevent the paste from making your fingers sticky – this could damage the neat surface of the modelled figures or shapes.

A selection of tools will be needed – see the section on marzipan modelling tools (page 97).

When complete the figures are best sprayed with cocoa butter to protect the marzipan from drying and provide a fine glaze. All marzipan work that has to be stored for

Comic vegetable figures

sale is best covered in a cocoa butter glaze. Do not use confectioner's varnish as this is not an edible food substance.

The weight of each figure is important. When producing these for sale, work out the weight of each piece and calculate the food cost, overheads and gross profit to ensure the selling price reflects the total cost of production. Keep figure work to a maximum of 180 g.

The completed figures can be boxed in small, clear, plastic cartons available from sundries suppliers. A ribbon or label of contents, i.e. ingredients, will complete this profitable product.

Elephant

Ingredients	
Pink marzipan	*125 g*

Prepare some pink-coloured marzipan and portion into two balls, one approximately 50 g the other 75 g. Using clean hands, roll the balls lightly in the palms of your hand to produce two clean spheres.

Body
Take the larger sphere and form a short cone shape at either end. Make a 20 mm cut to divide each end and flatten. One end will be the feet (rear legs), the other the front legs. Leave this to dry. Dip into melted chocolate and place on silicone paper to set.

Head
Using the smaller sphere, form a cone shape at one end, approximately 50 mm in length. Next form an indent in the widest part of the cone (as seen in the photograph to the right). Make a cut in this, approximately 15–20 mm, and open to form a 'v' shape. Lift up the shape and place the two cut flaps flat onto cling film or paper. Flatten to form the ear shapes (refer to photograph, steps 4, 5 and 6). Elongate the point of the cone shape and twist or bend to form the elephant's trunk. Using small fine scissors, make two small 'v' shaped cuts under the trunk for the tusks. Some white marzipan can be used to make two tusks. Press these into place and make certain they are securely attached.

Finally, dip the base of the head into melted chocolate and place onto the main body shape; allow to set.

Making a marzipan elephant

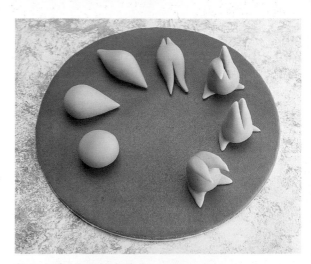

Steps to forming the body

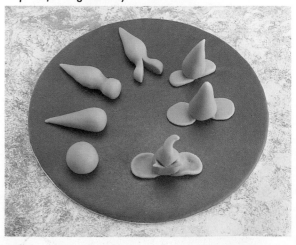

Steps to forming the head

Assemble and add the finishing details

Easter chicks

Ingredients	
Yellow marzipan	50 g
Red marzipan	15 g

Form two balls, one two-thirds larger than the other; join these with melted chocolate and dip the base. Press onto a silicone sheet. Roll out a piece of red marzipan 4 mm thick, using a ribboned box roller, and cut a diamond of paste. Attach this to the head with a ball tool to form the beak. Roll a straw of red paste and pucker to form a crest; place on the head. Pipe on eyes with royal icing and chocolate.

Duck

Ingredients	
White or cream-coloured marzipan	50 g
Pale orange marzipan	10 g

Portion as for the chick and form a ball with the smaller piece and a tapered carrot shape with the larger piece. Twist the tail of the body slightly upwards or sideways, and join the head with chocolate. To form the beak, roll out the orange paste as for the chick and cut two small circles. Attach to the head with a ball tool and pipe on the eyes. Finally, dip the base in chocolate.

Snail

Ingredients	
White marzipan	50 g
Brown or chocolate-coloured marzipan	20 g

Roll the white marzipan into a ball between your hands, lighten the moulding to produce a clean surface. Form a carrot shape and, from the thicker end, pull two small tapering shapes for the feelers/eyes of the snail. Roll the chocolate marzipan to form a thinner longer carrot shape and roll this up, starting from the thick end, to form the shell. Place the shell on the base, both dipped in a little couverture, and decorate the eyes with piping chocolate.

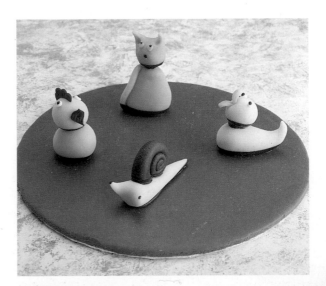

Marzipan animals

103

Hedgehog

Ingredients	
Brown marzipan	75 g

Roll a smooth ball of marzipan, then form it into a dumpy carrot shape. With fine scissors, cut spikes 15 mm from the tip back towards the thick end. Dip the whole piece in chocolate with a dipping tool; decorate the eyes in the usual manner.

■ PETITS FOURS FRUITS

Almond paste and marzipan have long been used for inclusion in the display of petits fours and sweetmeats for dinners, banquets and special functions. High class confectioners produce an array of marzipan sweetmeats, finished with fondant, chocolate and all kinds of decorations. It is best to use a quality marzipan paste such as Renmarz from J. F. Renshaw; this is mixed with glucose and icing sugar to produce an excellent modelling paste that keeps well (see page 97).

Petits fours without marzipan fruits

A selection of marzipan fruits

would not be petits fours. Simple shapes and colours are quickly produced to provide a selection of interesting sweetmeats for special dinners or functions. Christmas seems to be the popular time for such delicacies. Pastillage can be produced using a woven design box roller to form small baskets and handles to display either individual or multi-portion selections of small fruits. Each fruit should be no more than 10–15 g.

1 Prepare the selection of marzipan pastes by dividing the bulk basic paste into equal weights. Colour and flavour each portion according to the number of fruits being produced. The colour should be kept light and enhanced by spraying or painting to promote a natural finish. Wrap each prepared paste in clingfilm to prevent drying.

2 Clean the work surface well and ensure it is free from grease or dust. Roll the paste to form a long rope, approximately 15 mm thick, then divide the whole length into 15 mm pieces using a plastic scraper or knife – a blunt edge is preferred.

3 Mould each piece to form a basic round, oval, long or pear shape, depending on the fruit being produced.

Apple

Cut the rope, as described above, into 10 mm pieces. Using apple green colour and flavour, form as described above (page 96). Mould a ball, pressing the top slightly to create an apple shape; indent the top for the stalk. Dry for 1 hour and spray with red colour, using an aerograph. When you are used to spraying, a speckled finish is not difficult to produce. Press the spray button, quickly releasing it immediately to form a spotted coating on the fruits.

Take a small volume of brown marzipan for the stalk and join using the small ball tool.

Steps to making marzipan pears and oranges

Allow to dry overnight and store in a cool dry place, gently covered with a sheet of paper such as silicone.

Orange

Cut the rope into slightly larger pieces than that of the apple. Form all the pieces into round balls, then mould them into slightly oval shapes. Mark the outside of the fruit with a grater or sago board (sago glued to 2 pieces of wood between which the fruits are moulded to form the indented surface). Form the depression in the top and mark a series of small lines in the top. A serrated cone tool can produce this effect on the orange. Finish with a small green piece of marzipan cut using the small spring-loaded flower cutter. Do not use cloves to represent the calyx or stalk as this can be a health risk if swallowed. Glaze with cocoa butter spray or paint with cocoa butter, or spray with weak gum arabic solution.

Grapes

Produce either green or burgundy marzipan and form into 10 mm pieces. Divide each piece

into small pea-sized round or slightly oval shapes. Stick each small ball together as they are moulded, and so build up the grape bunch shape. Make a lighter brown stalk and a fine vine leaf. These are time consuming and only worth doing for display purposes or where small quantities are required.

Pear

Make some pale green or yellow paste, form a ball shape in your hands and re-shape to a pear shape, rolling lightly between the heel of your hands. Indent the top surface with a ball tool and dry. Spray with yellow, brown and red to provide an authentic pear finish. Finally, add the stalks which are best tapered slightly. Dry overnight.

Banana

Colour and flavour the banana marzipan. Cut the rope into 10 mm pieces and roll the pieces to form a tapered banana shape. Press the edges slightly to enhance the shape. Bend the banana and paint or spray on a fine amount of brown. Paint the ends with brown and green.

Strawberry

Prepare strawberry-coloured and flavoured paste, form into the rope and divide into 10 mm pieces. Shape all the pieces to form a round shape then, with the heel of your hand, form a cone shape resembling the strawberry. Roll each piece on the grater or sago boards. Add the calyx and stalk, cut from green marzipan using a star flower cutter. Roll in fine caster sugar or leave and just spray with cocoa butter.

Lemon

Use a primrose yellow paste. Divide the rope

into 10 mm pieces. Mould a round shape, then form this with your hands and fingers to produce a fat oval shape with tapered base and top. Mark the surface with a grater. Add the stalk, cut using a spring-loaded small flower cutter; use green/brown marzipan for this.

Plum

Using a red plum-coloured marzipan, form the rope and cut into 10 mm pieces. Roll these into a round, then oval plum shape. Again, the taper needs to be smooth. Add a small stalk. Yellow plums can also be produced and enhanced with a burgundy spray.

Peach

Make a ball of pale peach-coloured and flavoured paste. Mark a line indent from the top down the sides of the peach shape, dry and then lightly spray either side of the line with pink/red colour. Add an icing sugar bloom; do not, as some books suggest, use cornflour – this can create fermentation in the marzipan.

■ FLOWERS

Flowers made from sugar or flower paste – roses, carnations, daisies, sweet peas, lilies or campions – can be easily produced from marzipan. A little sugar paste or pastillage can be added to the almond paste to strengthen the flower. Use a cutter to form the base shape, and mould with finger and thumb to produce a fine edge or thin petal; allow to stand for a few minutes and construct the shape.

Petals can be joined with gum arabic or carefully blended with a ball tool. Flat Christmas roses or wild dog roses need to be supported; an apple or fruit polystyrene tray is ideal to nestle the flower until it is dry enough

to lift. The main use of marzipan flowers is for celebration cakes, tortes and gâteaux.

Producing a rose

1   Make some coloured paste in two shades, a deeper tone for the centre and paler shades for the outer petals.
2   Take the darker paste and form it into a carrot shape.
3   Thin one edge with the heel of your hand, then gently form the petal with either your fingers or a palette knife dusted with icing sugar.
4   Run the blade under the thinned edge to remove it from the work surface, pick the shape up and roll the thin edge to form the bud of the rose. Press the base to form the base of the bud and pull the fine edge out with a slight turn; place the bud down.
5   Take the dark shade of paste again and form rose petals, either with a cutter or by thinning the end of a carrot shape between your first finger and thumb. Place two petals opposite each other, folded completely around the bud, with the top of the petal pulled back slightly.
6   Next produce three petals from the paler shade of paste and interlink these around the bud and two petals; pull the petal edge to form a ripple fold indicative of a real flower (half rose). Add five more petals for a larger flower (full rose).
7   Add a green base to the rose and dry. Powdered colour can be used to highlight the flowers. It is better to make a number of buds and then the two petals, allowing the paste to dry slightly. Petals can droop when soft, so always place upright against the bud and fold back slightly to prevent the petal formation from opening too much. Once the flower dries, after 20 minutes or so, the petals can be opened more to enhance the overall effect. Rose leaves can

be made using plastic flexible leaf markers.

OTHER OBJECTS

Walls and brickwork and base surfaces

Shades of grey, black and brown marzipan can be used to create brick, stone or walls. Use a ball or paddle tool to mark the pattern of crazy paving – this will produce very good effects. Walls can be built in the conventional way: colour and roll the paste out on a flat surface, cut the tiny brick shapes and begin to build on top of your paving base. Arches and complete buildings can be made in this way.

Trees

Trees are more difficult to make but can be modelled from mixed brown, green and black shades. Build up the strength of the marzipan by keeping the base thick and thinning down as the tree is built. You could give it a face. Rub the pieces with a tool and your fingers to hide any joins completely.

Grass and heather

Grass can be made from coloured paste by pressing it through a fine nylon sieve. Remove the thin fine marzipan grass with an artist's small stepped palette knife, and place it over the edge of a path or wall to create an unusual surface. Small vines and ivy can be made and trailed on trees or over surfaces. Hide small insects in the mixed textured pastes.

Coloured paste can be forced through fine nylon or metal sieves, small amounts at a time: this produces a grass or heather effect for building up plant areas; flowers can then be added. Mixed colours work well; first push through some lilac-coloured paste then some green – the lilac is then joined to the top of the green to create a heather effect. Slice this from the sieve and place onto your model, secure in place with a cocktail stick.

Leaves, plaques and borders

A good range of leaf cutters can now be purchased from cake art suppliers. Pin marzipan between two pieces of plastic or clingfilm to get a smooth, thin sheet and cut the required number of leaves. These can be produced when you are quiet, to keep as a stock decoration for busier periods.

Marzipan plaques can be made using different colours and shapes as a gift, the centre of a novelty cake, or a simple oval with a message of endearment.

Borders of mottled multi-coloured edging can be made to enhance bar cakes and logs or incorporated in the designs of tortes. Individual pieces can be made to produce a symmetrical design image on cakes or as a simple addition to a cold dessert.

PIÈCES MONTÉES

Pictured is a piece modelled from coloured marzipan using Renshaw recipe no 1 (page 97). It shows how individual techniques have been used to create the whole piece. The scene is of novelty bears in a garden; hidden are small animals and insects, taking note of the ogres nearby. This type of piece takes many hours of modelling to create and is best carried out in the evening when it is quiet.

Pièce Montée: bear garden

1   Select a suitable base on which to model your work; use a non-standard shape to add to the overall image of the piece. Work on the base first to produce a stone and grass effect. Then decide where each group of figures will be sited and triangulate their position in relation to trees or key viewing points of the model. The piece should look good from all angles. Above all, if you have a good base of mottled stone, wall and path to build on, then this will enhance the overall picture of the model.

2   Next add any larger pieces such as trees and rock formations, Add, for example, a face blended into a tree or rock; create interest so that, like a walk through a secret garden, the viewer always comes upon something different to keep the attention fixed. Grass and heather-type effects are easily achieved by pressing a coloured marzipan paste through a fine nylon sieve with your thumbs. The marzipan is then removed with a small stepped palette knife and placed into position. Neaten any pieces which do not blend with a needle or cocktail stick.

3   Leave the major base work at this point and concentrate on preparing the coloured paste for each novelty bear: a picture will assist in the identification of each colour required. Wrap each colour individually before any modelling of the figure begins.

4   Work on each character in turn; study the photograph on page 109 to identify the shape and size of each piece. When formed, each should be carefully wrapped in two or three layers of film and stored until all the fine animal work is complete. Remember, the judge will look for work which incorporates saleable-sized figures.

Novelty bear

5   Next make a selection of butterflies, frogs, ladybirds, snakes, spiders, beetles and moles to be hidden among the shrubs, bushes and rocks; these will add to the skill of the piece and create interest. The gummy berry bushes can be laden with tiny fruits and the ogres can be made to look ugly and friendly or ugly and fierce.

When all pieces have been formed then glaze the base well or dull the finish with a dust and rubbing action using fine bride cake icing sugar. The judges will inspect for dust, marks, fingerprints and oiling of the paste – they will expect a super-clean finish to your work. Each piece can be sprayed with cocoa butter spray or brushed using a very fine brush with melted cocoa butter; keep this warm over a night light. Do not use a thick layer of cocoa butter as this can set and give a poor covering. Finally, secure each separate piece in position, ensuring they are firmly held to prevent damage during transportation. Arrange the figures to portray a story or scene, as found in the actual cartoon. Wrap the finished model in layers of clingfilm. A pouch of film can protect delicate items for transport. Cover the complete piece to prevent dust or dirt spoiling the surfaces.

■ CAKES AND ALMOND CONFECTIONERY

Covering fruit and celebration cakes

Marzipan, almond paste or covering pastes are used to cover sponge or fruit cakes before

Coating a cake with almond paste

decoration with either royal icing or sugar paste. To ensure the finished cake is balanced, the paste must be pinned and joined to produce flat, neat surfaces.

Traditionally, marzipan was fairly thick, with a layer up to 25 mm not uncommon; today the covering is usually about 5–10 mm, due to cost. Fruit cakes need to be matured and fed with a mix of warm stock syrup and rum or brandy.

1 Trim the sponge or fruit cake to produce a flat shape.
2 Wipe down any crumbs to prevent the surface of the paste being spoilt.
3 Take some softened marzipan and roll out to a thickness of 8–10 mm; dust with icing sugar to prevent the paste from sticking.
4 Boil some apricot purée and water and brush this over the base of the cake.
5 Place the cake onto the paste and trim round, holding the knife perpendicular to the work surface; remove trimmings.
6 Roll out and cut a length of paste, having measured the outer surface with a strip of paper.
7 Re-boil the apricot jam and brush the sides of the cake well.
8 Roll up the marzipan and place around the cake; trim with a small sharp blade and carefully seal any joins.
9 Firm the sides and surface with a flat-edged scraper to ensure a flat surface before leaving to dry.
10 A single-tiered cake can be decorated within 12 hours, but multi-tiered cakes are best left for 48 hours prior to coating with icing or paste: this allows the almond paste to dry and form a firm surface.

Note: If a fruit cake is sealed correctly with the boiled apricot purée then the cake is preserved, provided it is stored in the correct conditions. Take care when using the boiled jam: it is very hot and can cause a nasty burn. Always have some iced water to hand in case of an accident when using boiled sugar solutions.

Simnel cake

The Simnel cake, it is said, has its origins in the time of King Henry VII, who ended the Wars of the Roses by marrying Elizabeth of York, so uniting the Lancaster and York Houses. Lambert Simnel, the son of an Oxford baker, was one of the pretenders to the throne in the following York uprising. After defeat, Simnel was given a pardon and subsequently worked as a baker in the Royal household. He shaped a special cake in the form of a crown to please his Royal master – the Simnel cake.

Ingredients	
Butter	450 g
Dark soft brown sugar	450 g
Egg	560 g
Soft flour	560 g
Ground almonds	100 g
Sultanas	450 g
Currants	675 g
Mixed peel	340 g
Mixed spice	28 g
Rum	28 ml
Colour as required	

Prepare all the fruit. Use the sugar batter method. Line four 15 cm tins or hoops. Pour in 250 g of the mixture and level. Place 250 g of flat marzipan on top and add a further 250 g of mixture. Bake at 180°C, protecting with silicone paper. Cool and remove the lining paper. Decorate the top with a crimped marzipan layer, joined with boiling apricot purée. Form a decorative edge or crimp and brush well with a mix of egg yolk and cream. Flash in the oven to glaze and colour the markings. Wash the top with a gum arabic solution and finish with decorative pastel fondant, piped beading or decoration, preserved confits or Easter motifs.

Battenburg designs

Battenburg cake is a fine sponge best made from high ratio sheet sponge – pink, white, yellow or green. The recipe is provided below. Cut the sponge into strips of square or triangle shapes and join with a fine raspberry or apricot purée. Care needs to be taken as high ratio sponges are very fragile, though they do have a good shelf life.

Roll out some almond or marzipan paste to 4 mm thickness. Spread a layer of jam onto the marzipan and wrap the joined strips of sponge. Roll up and neaten the oblong shape with marzipan scrapers. Crimp the top surface with pastry crimpers and pipe with fondant. Decorate as preferred.

HIGH RATIO SHEET SPONGE

Stage 1	
High ratio flour	560 g
Baking powder	40 g
High ratio fat	425 g

Blend for 3 minutes on a slow mixing speed or until a smooth paste results. Scrape down the sides of the bowl well.

Stage 2	
Caster sugar	740 g
Salt	14 g
Milk	225 ml
Colour and flavour	

Dissolve the above ingredients together and add to the mixture produced at stage 1 – do this slowly over 1 minute on slow speed. Scrape down well, then mix for a further 2 minutes on speed 2.

Stage 3	
Whole liquid egg	468 g
Milk	200 ml

Mix the egg and milk and add slowly to the mixture over 1 minute. Scrape down. Mix for a further 2 minutes on slow speed. The batter temperature needs to be 21°C. Place on a silicone-lined baking sheet and bake at 193–204°C for 30–40 minutes.

High ratio sponge works on the principle of fine fractionation of the flour particles using fully bleached flour. The flour has a particle size of between 20–30 microns, smaller than that of plain flour. The increased surface area allows more liquid to be held in the mixture. High ratio fat is superglycerinated and fully hydrogenated to balance the high liquid content of the recipe. Careful production methods need to be employed, but the resultant sponge is high quality, has a long shelf life and shapes well. Use the sponge a day old to aid cutting: the crumb structure is very fragile because of its fineness.

Koenigsburg marzipan

Use round or oval cutters to cut marzipan bouchées from raw marzipan or almond paste. Crimp or decorate the top edge with a pattern, and brush with a dextrin wash. Fill the centres with nougat and jam and pipe over flavoured coloured fondant. Finish with couverture and decorate with a cherry or glacé fruit. Other shapes such as those used for English rout biscuits can be made, glazed and decorated with crystallised fruits.

Almond biscuits

■ FINISHING MARZIPAN PRODUCTS

Cocoa butter spray, confectioner's varnish and gum arabic

Cocoa butter provides an ideal coating for marzipan goods. Melted and brushed thinly over the paste, it provides a protective glaze to prevent the items from drying. Cocoa butter spray can be purchased in spray form, and it provides an effective glaze and finish to figures, exhibition work or the everyday range of almond sweetmeats. Confectioner's varnish can still be purchased in litre units. It can only be used for display purposes and should never be used on food items for sale, as it is not edible.

The varnish can be applied after the mar-zipan pieces have dried. Use a soft brush and do not shake the varnish before application as this causes air bubbles to form which are difficult to remove. Brush an even coat over the display piece and leave to dry in a room where people will not pass, otherwise dust will be deposited on the surface and spoil the finish. It is a good idea to work late at night, when it is quiet and the air is still. Gum arabic powder, mixed with hot water and a small quantity of gin, is very good for sticking flower work together, joining pieces of a small figure or model or covering as a glaze. Use while still warm.

Spraying and tinting

AEROGRAPHS
Spraying or tinting marzipan work needs to be carefully executed. An aerograph can be pur-

chased from art suppliers for about £30 and this will do adequately for everyday spraying. Mix the colour and test it on cardboard first to set the action of the spray head; adjust if necessary. Do not spray near other work; always move items to be sprayed to a clean area of the kitchen as the spray does spread. Spray one or two coats which are very light; a quick press of the button will produce a speckled finish for oranges, apples and pears.

COLOUR TINTING

Using a good artist's brush, tint or lustre colours can be used to highlight figure work, flowers or template cutouts. Use tint with discretion: too much will destroy the effect. Always tint lightly; more can be added but not always taken away.

Tricks of the trade – secrets of fine work

Cleanliness of all equipment and surfaces is essential; wash your hands as often as you can to prevent the paste from sticking. Freeze your tools to produce a quality surface on competition work. Use cocoa butter to glaze the pieces. Modelling blocks for fruits can be purchased for scale production of fruits. Buy a small air gun to create a good natural finish on petit four fruit and vegetables. Build up your tool set and keep them wrapped in clingfilm to prevent damage or scratching. Make only the best quality paste for high class work and invest time, patience and a sense of humour in your work – you will need it.

5 CHOCOLATE

A selection of chocolates displayed under a chocolate lamp

INTRODUCTION

Chocolate is a firm favourite of many children and adults; the taste, range and variety of chocolate products tempt us all. It is one of the few products that in times of recession not only maintains its share of the confectionery market but actually extends sales. Used for confectionery, desserts, treats and complex *pièce montée* work, chocolate offers the modern artist a unique medium. The simple basic mixtures have the most complex structures, which even today require research to determine the large numbers of different fat crystal structures. Mixtures can be basic compound chocolates made from vegetable oils and fats, or real couverture (covering) chocolate made from blends of cocoa butter, milk solids, cocoa mass and sugar.

The history of chocolate is a subject in itself and we can only touch on its complexity; production has been modernised, using technology and, where once labour was used, machines are now employed. The expert chocolatier, though, is the only one who can manipulate, form and create art with chocolate. The finish of a torte, the quiff of a motif or the splendour of hand-dipped centres all require a great deal of knowledge and skill. This skill is finding a new life with young confectioners and pâtissiers seeking to master the principles and processes essential to chocolate art.

Origins

Although chocolate manufacture has only been developed in Europe during the previous 150 years or so, its great value as a food commodity has been known for many centuries. In AD 600 the Mayas migrated from central America deep into South America to establish the earliest known cocoa plantations. The Mayas and Aztecs used the beans to make a bitter drink mixed with spices which they called *cacahuatl*, meaning bitter water.

Columbus was the first European to discover the cocoa bean, in 1502, but it was Cortez, after conquering part of Mexico in 1519, who finally returned to Spain with his prize plunder, called *tchocolatl*. The Mexicans had given the cocoa tree a name meaning 'the food of the gods', for the Mexicans considered it a divine product. The Spaniards, however, had more practical ideas. They kept it a close secret, and so managed to keep the monopoly for over 100 years, after which it slowly spread to Italy, Holland and France.

The English gentry were introduced to drinking chocolate in 1657 when the first chocolate house opened in London. In 1828 a Dutchman called van Houten discovered a way to press the cocoa butter out of the chocolate mass and cocoa powder resulted. It was not until 1847 that J. S. Fry produced the first eating chocolate. One of the main production phases in chocolate production, called 'conching', was invented by the famous Rudolphe Lindt (1855–1909). This enabled cocoa butter to be added to chocolate, a method still used today. The conching of the cocoa butter and chocolate mass produced the melting quality so essential to produce fine quality chocolate.

BOTANY

The cocoa tree will grow to a height of 20–30 feet and requires some shade from larger forest trees. Usually, the seedling will reach a height of between 3–5 ft each year, producing on average 3–5 side branches. This pattern is repeated until the height of maturity is reached.

The flowers are about 1 cm in width and form on the lower branches and trunk. They are bi-sexual, do not have nectar or perfume and the pollen is too sticky to be dispersed by wind. A small midge is thought to be responsible for pollination. Many flowers are produced but only a very small number of these will be pollinated to develop into pods.

The pods take about 5–6 months to mature and are botanically classed as a berry. They are about 18–24 cm in length and 8–10 cm wide. The pod will contain somewhere between 15–35 seeds, held in a mucilaginous pulp when ripe. The pods do not have a natural method of opening and reproduction occurs by mammals, monkeys or squirrels eating the pulp and rejecting the seeds.

Practically all varieties can be categorised into two groups: Criolla and Forastero cocoas. The pure variety of Criolla is found mainly in Equador and Venezuela. This type is prone to climate changes and proves difficult to cultivate. The seeds of the Criolla are of a finer quality than those of the Forastero, they have a fine mild aroma and form the basis of the very best quality chocolate. They account for around 10% of the world's harvest. The remaining 90% of this harvest comes from the family of the cocoa tree, Forastero, which has many hybrids. The main growing areas are Brazil and West Africa. This hardy, heavy-cropping tree produces a bitter, harsher form of cocoa. The cocoa ranges from fine to medium and is either selected or blended according to the purpose and final product use. West Africa produces about 74% of the world's cocoa; North, Central and South America produce about 20%; Asia providing the remainder.

◼ PLANT TO PRODUCT

The ripe cocoa pods are removed from the tree and split open. Inside is found between 15–35 seeds (beans) in 5 distinct rows, surrounded by a soft pulp. The beans have an almond shape and vary in appearance depending on the variety.

The finer quality Criolla beans, when opened, have a yellow-white colour due to the absence of pigment. The Forastero bean, in contrast, has a deep-purplish colour. The beans and pulp of the pod are removed and taken to be stored in the fermentary. Cocoa trees will not bear fruit of any use until the fourth year of growth. The average crop or yield from a single tree will produce about 800–900 g of beans.

Fermentation

This stage in the life of the cocoa bean is the most important, for it is here that the cocoa develops the characteristic flavour of chocolate. The fermentation process will vary from region to region. Some growing areas will place the beans in heaps or mounds, covered with banana leaves or branches; others will place the beans and pulp in special baskets or large boxes. Now covered, the beans and pulp are left to ferment for 2–6 days, again dependent on the variety and region of origin. During this crucial period the beans are turned over a number of times to be certain that all the beans and pulp ferment.

During the fermentation process the pulp-bearing sugar and beans as a mass ferments and develops temperatures up to 50°C. This ensures that the beans do not germinate and the astringent and bitter tastes mellow as new substances develop.

These new substances are the precursors of the aroma components from which the true cocoa perfume later develops, particularly during the stages of drying and roasting.

Enzymes are released by these substances, which degrade proteins to peptides and amino-acids; hydrolysation of the anthocyanines and oxidation of the polyphenols also results.

Little is known about the complex chemical processes involved, but without fermentation the cocoa beans will not develop a good rich flavour when roasted. The Criolla bean turns a yellow-brown colour and the Forastero a violet-brown.

Drying

The fermented beans at this stage will still contain about 55–60% water, which needs to be reduced. Drying methods vary from region to region; some beans are sun-dried on mats, while others use fires. More advanced production uses mechanical driers. The water content needs to be reduced to about 4%, resulting in a darker colour with the flavour being enhanced. The beans are now packed into sacks and shipped to Europe and North America.

Roasting

The beans are checked for their quality and then undergo a thorough cleaning process to remove any stalks or foreign material that might remain.

Now the bean is ready to be roasted. This is carried out in furnaces which reach a temperature of 130°C. The beans pass over a conveyor system for a period of 15–20 minutes; the bean is heated to 115–121°C when producing cocoa powder and 99–104°C when required for chocolate.

When roasting a blend of fermented beans, undesirable compounds (volatile organic acids) are first removed, reaction then occurs between amino-acids, peptides and reducing sugars. This phase results in an important change. Where the Maillard reaction occurs, reducing sugars and amino-compounds react to cause non-enzymic browning essential to the flavour in chocolate. Following this the polymerisation adds to the brown colour with the formation of melanoidins, with flavour compounds occurring at the same time. Roasting requires great skill to produce the very best results in both colour and flavour.

Crushing and shelling

Roasting assists in the loosening of the husk or shell as then the beans are broken (winnowed) into pieces called nibs. They pass through a series of rollers and sieves to achieve this size. The husks are used by the chemical industry and the nibs are made into chocolate. Chocolate quality is determined in part by the extraction rate of the dust and husk particles.

Blending

Some cocoa processors will blend different beans once the cleaning stage is completed; some wait until the nibs have been sized. Each producer guards the secret of their particular quality blend. The blending stage is again crucial in determining the flavour and quality of the cocoa product, especially for plain chocolate.

Flavour analysis and mixing

The overall flavour of cocoa is determined by the volatile and non-volatile compounds and is complex in nature. Sensitive equipment is used by chemists to analyse such components. Some 400 different-flavoured compounds have been discovered, although only about 200 have been identified. Cocoa flavour is a very complex combination, which has not been successfully reproduced by synthetic methods.

Bitter compounds are a constituent of cocoa, especially those of theobromine and caffeine, thought to produce headaches or migraine in some consumers. Other bitter compounds are formed during roasting from proteins, e.g. diketopiperazine. The astringency of the cocoa flavour, particularly noticeable in non-alkalized cocoa powder, is caused by tannins.

Grinding

Here, the pre-ground cocoa nibs are conveyed into special milling machines and fed onto rollers where they are ground to produce a fine paste. The heat produced from such pressure melts the cocoa butter (50% of the bean), resulting in a thick liquid mixture. The thick liquid has a dark brown colour and a strong odour characteristic in chocolate. As it cools, it sets to form cocoa paste. The quality of the finished product depends on the fineness of the cocoa particles.

COCOA POWDER

Cocoa powder can be produced by 3 different methods:

1 *Liquor process:* Here the nib is hot ground to form a fluid mass which sets on cooling and can be moulded. Cocoa butter results from the hot mass being hydraulically pressed, either before or subsequent to 'alkalization'. The fat content is reduced from 55% to between 12 and 25%, according to how the cocoa is to be used. The remaining mass is now called 'press cake'; this is ground and sieved to form cocoa powder.

2 *Nib alkalization or Dutch process:* Strong alkali is used to soak the nibs until all the solution is absorbed. The wet nib is then dried and ground to form a liquor then pressed hydraulically. This process produces a much darker and richer colour.

3 *Extrusion or expeller process:* Steam is used to soften the nibs which are fed into an expeller press where the fat content is reduced to around 10%. This press system tears the nibs and cake results. Again, this is processed into cocoa powder.

COCOA BUTTER

Grinding is the normal stage where cocoa butter is pressed from the nib. In Britain, cocoa butter is defined as the fat which is obtained from the cocoa beans by hydraulic or expeller pressing, or by solvent extraction. Cocoa butter is light yellow with a very brittle fracture below 20°C. It melts at around 35°C and softens at between 30–32°C.

Cocoa butter is used to thin chocolate couverture and, when mixed with an equal quantity, is called 'velour', used primarily for decorative purposes. It is the main ingredient of white chocolate, but is also important in plain and milk chocolate, adjusting the properties of both.

Refining

The chocolate mass is completely mixed with a high-grade, finely pulverised sugar, free from any traces of moisture or invert sugar which can cause problems during this stage in production; all are mixed in a blending kettle. Cocoa butter is added and blending takes place to produce the required consistency – a skilled task.

The mixture is then sent between refining rollers which reduces the size of the non-fat particles to ensure the chocolate will be smooth. The colour of the chocolate becomes lighter at this stage as air is incorporated. Volatile residues are released at this blending stage and any small elements of moisture left are evaporated.

Conching

This strange name comes from the Latin *conche*, meaning shell. Conching is the mechanical agitation of the chocolate mass, and additional cocoa butter is added at this stage. Again, any volatile substances are removed and, at a temperature of 60–70°C, the added cocoa butter and mass are mixed, developing the flavour.

Conching takes a long time – 10–24 hours for milk chocolate, 24–96 hours for plain chocolate. Any additional flavours are mixed in at this stage in the process before being run off from the conche tank and set. The chocolate is then called *couverture* or 'covering chocolate'.

Types of chocolate

PLAIN COUVERTURE
Plain couverture ranges from very bitter, high-quality grades to cheaper grades. All need to be tempered. Plain couverture is a mixture of cocoa mass, sugar and cocoa butter. The recipe for each grade of plain couverture will differ according to its use – this will be reflected in the price per kilo.

MILK CHOCOLATE
The process is the same as for plain couverture chocolate, described previously, but milk is added at the refining stage and the conche is carried out at a lower temperature.

Milk chocolate contains about 1.5% moisture, and full cream milk containing up to 12.5% of milk solids including fat. One of 3 methods are employed to remove the moisture (87.5%) from the milk:

1 Milk powder process: Milk powder is mixed with cocoa liquor, sugar, cocoa butter, lecithin and flavour.

2 Block milk process: This is a form of sweetened condensed milk where the water is heat evaporated to produce a milk–water content of 8% and 45% sugar content; this is not employed so widely and the use of condensed milk is minimal.

3 Crum process: This development revolutionised the manufacture of milk chocolate. Fresh milk is filtered and pre-heated to 75°C where concentration occurs of between 30–40%. These solids have sugar added and dissolved, then the mix is sent to a condensing chamber under vacuum where the mix is boiled. This continues at 75°C until concentration is at 90% and the sugar demonstrates signs of crystallisation.

This product is now mixed with cocoa mass, blended and dried. Finally, cocoa butter is added and the mixture continues to be processed as for plain couverture to develop the smoothness and flavour.

WHITE CHOCOLATE
White chocolate is made from a blend of cocoa butter, sugar and milk powder, or white crumb chocolate and cocoa butter, instead of chocolate liquor. White chocolate requires a milder flavour of cocoa butter, preferably one that is deodorised, pressed from a lightly roasted bean. White chocolate produced from the crumb base has better keeping qualities. White chocolate – along with other chocolate coatings that do not contain cocoa – is prone to oxidative rancidity if exposed to light. White chocolate will also pick up odour or flavour from other commodities. Some people believe it should not be called chocolate because it contains no cocoa solids.

BAKER'S CHOCOLATE
Plain baker's or cooking chocolate, as it is sometimes called, is available in button, tablet or block form and does not require 'tempering'. For general use a safe melting temperature should not exceed 46°C. Baker's chocolate has a high fat content and is relatively cheap and versatile. It is used for decoration, fillings and coatings. Baker's chocolate can be easily cut to form shapes

when cold and makes excellent *copeaux au chocolat*.

STORAGE OF CHOCOLATE AND CHOCOLATE PRODUCTS

Optimum storage conditions

Chocolate is an expensive commodity and requires correct storage conditions to preserve its flavour and quality. Chocolate goods can easily be spoilt if packed or stored incorrectly. The importance of strict attention to temperature and humidity conditions during storage cannot be over-stressed. Too high or low a temperature is to be avoided, as well as a varying temperature. Chocolate will produce a bloom under these conditions.

If the atmosphere is too moist then condensation and absorption might occur, resulting in a 'greying' effect on the chocolate.

The ideal storage temperature for chocolate is between 16–18°C, with a low humidity. A dry room will be ideal for storage but needs to be warmed in cold weather conditions – it is essential to maintain the temperatures constant. A well-ventilated room is important with sufficient air space between shelving for circulation of air. Never store chocolate or chocolate products near other flavours or strong-smelling food items: these will taint the chocolate.

Problems during storage

The bloom that appears on chocolate which has been poorly stored can also result from inadequate handling whilst the chocolate is in a liquid form.

Fat bloom: This results when the chocolate is too warm and appears as white streaks on the surface of the chocolate.

Sugar bloom: This is a white bloom which appears on the chocolate surface as a result of the liquid chocolate being used at too low a temperature.

Checking for quality upon delivery

When delivered, chocolate should be checked for evidence of damage, sugar or fat bloom or graining – this is a white sugar grain evident in old or badly stored chocolate. Many companies do not understand the critical nature of temperature and humidity when storing these products.

Always purchase from a specialist who sells only chocolate or confectionery goods. If faults are discovered the whole order needs to be returned. The high cost of bulk purchasing means that a careful inspection of the order must be made before it is accepted. Deal with the same supplier when you are satisfied with the quality of chocolate supplied. Quality is determined by the grade and price paid. Check the wrappings, boxes or cartons to ensure no damage is evident, also check your storage temperatures and humidity levels prior to and during storage.

TEMPERING

The term 'tempering' is used in many different industries to denote the heat processing of a material to bring it to the desired crystalline state. This applies to chocolate couverture – couverture is tempered so that the final solidified product will have all the properties of a particular crystalline form:

1 A good gloss
2 A hard surface
3 A good shelf life
4 No bloom (fat or sugar)
5 A brittle snap when fractured

133

Composition – fat crystal structures

Couverture is a suspension of sugar particles in cocoa butter. The sugar and cocoa particles do not affect the problem of tempering, as they remain solid at all normal temperatures; it is the cocoa butter that needs to be considered. Cocoa butter can occur in six different polymorphic states with a melting point from 17.3°C to 36.4°C.

We need to consider four key polymorphic forms to understand the complex nature of the tempering function in using couverture.

y form: This is produced by very rapid cooling of the liquid fats. Its melting point is approximately 17°C; this is very unstable and transforms quickly, even at low temperatures, to the x form.

x form: This has a melting point of approximately 21–24°C.

b^1 *form:* The x form changes at normal temperatures to the b^1 form, with a melting point of approximately 27–29°C.

b form: Ultimately the b form results which has a stable nature with a melting point of approximately 34–35°C.

These four polymorphic forms become the two key fat crystal forms, A and B; which need to be processed correctly to ensure the tempering process is correct.

Put simply, the process changes as y and x become A, and b^1 becomes B. The B type crystal is stable and the one to which type A fat crystal will transform. Because type A is not stable, it has a lower melting point with a lower latent heat than the stable B which melts more easily. Because the cocoa butter fat crystal A has a low melting point it feels greasy to the touch at room temperatures.

If the chocolate crystallises incorrectly with the cocoa butter in the form of A fat crystals, then it will slowly transform to the stable B state, but in doing so produces all the characteristics of badly tempered chocolate, i.e. surface streaks and blotches.

If the cocoa butter fat crystal develops in the B stable form initially, then the resultant finish will be glossy, and the mass will set and shrink to produce a good snap to the chocolate. The prime aim therefore is to produce the stable B crystal form and not the unstable A crystal form of cocoa fat crystals.

The formation of crystals from a liquid involves the arrangement of the molecules of the liquid in a precise or definite pattern. A crystals have one pattern, while the B crystals have a different pattern. The cooling of liquid cocoa butter will give a mixture of A and B which needs to be avoided. If, however, cocoa butter is cooled until it is just about to begin to set or solidify and a small quantity of B crystal is added, then the liquid mass will eventually crystallise in the form of the B fat crystal. The reason for this is that the liquid will use the existing pattern as a template. By making use of the varying temperatures of the cocoa butter, it is possible to obtain both type A and type B crystals. Bring the chocolate to a complete liquid state at 49°C stirring slowly, then reduce the temperature to 28°C – then some of the cocoa butter will solidify, giving a mixture of both A and B crystals.

The A crystals melt at approximately 28°C, whereas the B crystals do not melt until a temperature of 34°C is reached. If, therefore, the couverture is heated up to 31°C all the A crystals of fat will melt and leave only the B crystals; thus the chocolate is said to be 'tempered'.

The working temperature range of plain chocolate is just below the solidification point of the B crystal; a safe temperature is 31–32°C

For milk chocolate this is about 29–31°C. This is different because of the milk fat which is softer than the cocoa butter fat and melts at a lower temperature.

Temperatures for plain, milk and white chocolate

Chocolate that has not been tempered in the correct way will present problems of fat and sugar bloom. It may also not set when moulded to form eggs. Tempering aids the solidification of the cocoa fat crystal which results in the mass setting quickly in a fine crystalline form. The fat trace is sometimes called the 'grain'. If tempering is not correctly carried out then the fat crystals set slowly in a larger crystalline pattern. This results in chocolate with a poor gloss and an inconsistent finish.

To temper the chocolate correctly, it needs to be slowly and thoroughly mixed to distribute the grain. If not stirred well, the chocolate can set with a streaky finish.

Plain chocolate: Break the chocolate into small pieces to aid melting, and place in a double boiler, porringer or clean stainless steel bowl. If using a double jacket pan, the water should be hot but not boiling.

Warm the chocolate, stirring regularly and slowly to melt the complete mass to 45–47°C. Melting should be done slowly. Cool the chocolate down to 27°C, then warm to a working temperature of 30°C.

Milk chocolate: Prepare the chocolate by melting carefully to no more than 43°C, avoiding any contact with moisture which will ruin the couverture. Melt and stir the chocolate slowly, cool to 27°C, then warm slightly to achieve a working temperature of 29–30°C.

White chocolate: White chocolate is made from cocoa butter, sugar and milk powder and is prepared by tempering as for couverture. Always check the temperatures recommended by the manufacturer as these can vary slightly depending on the grade and quality of the chocolate.

Tempering

Once the mass is melted and slowly stirred, the tempering can be achieved by a number of methods. This applies only to couverture or covering chocolate as described above, not to baker's chocolate which is dealt with on page 125.

Slab method: The couverture is melted to 45–47°C, stirring continuously and slowly. Pour between $\frac{1}{2}$ and $\frac{2}{3}$ onto a clean marble slab and work the couverture using a clean scraper or large palette knife. The chocolate must be moved slowly and constantly to keep an equal temperature until it begins to thicken or solidify. As soon as it begins to thicken, transfer this chocolate back into the remaining warm chocolate and stir slowly and thoroughly. Refer to the working temperature for each individual type of chocolate.

Cooling method: Melt the couverture in the usual way, preferably in a double pan; the outer pan should contain hot but not boiling water. Remove the inner pan and place in a bowl of iced water. Stir the chocolate slowly until it begins to set. Return the pan to the hot water and warm carefully to the working temperature stirring continuously. If at any time the temperature of the chocolate is permitted to go above 33°C, then the couverture must be re-tempered (i.e. cooled to its lower temperature and re-warmed to its working temperature).

Equipment for tempering

A tempering kettle, or porringer as it is usually called, is useful where chocolate is used frequently. The porringer is usually a double-jacketed pan, electric and made of stainless steel. Older round porringers were made of copper and a heater warmed the water sealed between the inner and outer pans. The porringer is filled with broken small pieces of chocolate. The modern stainless steel porringer can be purchased in various sizes and is rectangular in shape. These are thermostically heat-controlled to maintain the tempered chocolate at its working temperature.

Once a mass of chocolate is tempered then, as it is used, more block chocolate can be added. The tempered mass will seed the addi-

Porringer and dipping forks

tional chocolate. This method is used for enrobing machines where a continuous need for tempered chocolate exists. A tank of tempered chocolate sits underneath the enrober conveyor and chocolate is recycled once collected from the agitation of the coated centres.

Enrobers are used in volume production where large quantities of chocolates are covered. The machine can be a small unit for small-scale production of specialist chocolates to supply designer chocolate businesses, or large tunnel enrobers used for mass production for the retail market. The enrober is essentially a continuous belt which holds the centres and moves through a stream of chocolate, covering and agitating the centres at the same time. The reason for this is to both cover the centre evenly and to remove excess chocolate. It is critical that the centres reach a temperature of 21°C before being covered; this also applies to hand-dipped centres. Otherwise, if the centre is too warm or too cold, the finish of the tempered chocolate will be affected.

Handling liquid chocolate – possible problems

Chocolate is a complex commodity, used and consumed in large quantities daily. If not handled carefully it can create costly problems. Correct tempering is a basic technique which must be mastered before any chocolate work can be produced. No art can replace the sheen and quality of well-tempered couverture. Temperature is crucial to this process – take account of the location, weather conditions, and humidity. If you work at or near sea level, humidity can be a problem when working with sugar, icing, chocolate or marzipan.

Centres to be covered with chocolate need to be warm, but if too warm then the couverture will run off and not set. If centres are too cold, they will have a dull finish when covered. Covered centres should not be subjected to very cool temperatures; 18–19°C is suitable.

Damp and moisture will spoil chocolate, therefore store chocolate and chocolate products in a dry place. Avoid allowing any moisture to contact the chocolate (except when piping chocolate is being prepared). Excess humidity or a damp atmosphere can spoil chocolate very quickly; water and steam have a similar effect if in contact with the chocolate. Chocolate is affected when the humidity exceeds 75% or above.

VARIETIES OF CHOCOLATE

Couverture and compound

It is important to understand the difference between couverture and cheaper compound or baker's chocolates. Couverture is made from processed cocoa butter, cocoa mass (cocoa and cocoa butter) and sugar, with the addition of milk solids for milk chocolate. Compound or baker's chocolate, however, is not made with a cocoa butter fat but a hydrogenated fat and lecithin stabilizer. Some grades of coating chocolate may contain small amounts of cocoa butter.

Because baker's chocolate does not contain cocoa butter, tempering is not required. The covering chocolate can be melted up to 43°C; if exceeded, the coating may spoil – sugar crystals form to granulate the mix and this can then not be used other than for flavouring butter creams. Care must be taken with regard to moisture, steam and humidity if good results are to be achieved.

Because baker's chocolate does not contain cocoa butter, it is less expensive than couverture. It also tends to be more flexible with less snap than that of couverture. Designs and cut-outs are easily produced using cutters or templates. The coating can be cut, when cold, to form shapes, bases or decorative pieces for torten or desserts. This type of chocolate is available in milk, white and plain and as a block, tablets or thinner slabs. It is used for masking biscuits, whipping as a decoration and, generally, as a cheap substitute for the real thing.

High grade–low grade chocolate recipes

The development of a recipe for chocolate should be based on three criteria:

1 The intended market use.
2 The limitation on material and production costs.
3 The desired quality.

Many different recipes are therefore used. There are also many processing differences within a recipe which will alter flavour, such as:

1 Type of bean used.
2 Degree of roast of the bean.
3 Treatment of the milk, e.g. level of caramelisation.
4 Chocolate crumb or milk powder base.
5 Blend of butters.
6 Additional flavours, e.g. vanillin and use of emulsifiers.

The level of fat within the recipe is normally determined by the processing requirements, i.e. a lower viscosity chocolate is required for covering than moulding. Most chocolate recipes contain a small quantity of lecithin which will reduce the chocolate viscosity for similar fat contents. The UK chocolate regulations allow the addition of 5% vegetable fat, whereas European legislation requires all the fat to be cocoa butter. The selection of vegetable fat is quite critical in that it must be cocoa-butter-compatible and not adversely affect the hardness. A typical vegetable fat used with chocolate would be Coberine.

The following recipes were supplied by Mr Alan Booth, NPD and Process Engineering Manager, Cadbury Ltd.

HIGH COCOA SOLIDS (BITTER) CHOCOLATE

Ingredients	
Cocoa liquor	70%
Sugar	30%
No lecithin required as high fat content	

ORDINARY DARK CHOCOLATE

Ingredients	
Cocoa liquor	45%
Cocoa butter	7.7%
Sugar	47%
Lecithin	0.3%

MILD DARK CHOCOLATE – UK TYPE

Ingredients	
Cocoa liquor	35%
Cocoa butter	7%
Vegetable fat	5%
Sugar	52.7%
Lecithin	0.3%

MILK CHOCOLATE – CONTINENTAL TYPE

Ingredients	
Cocoa liquor	14%
Full cream milk powder	16%
Cocoa butter	22.7%
Sugar	47%
Lecithin	0.3%

MILK CHOCOLATE – UK TYPE

Ingredients	
Cocoa liquor	10%
Full cream milk powder	23%
Cocoa butter	18%
Vegetable fat	5%
Sugar	43.7%
Lecithin	0.3%

CHOCOLATE TECHNIQUES

Moulding

A good clean and polished mould should always be used for moulding chocolate. Moulds can be made from any rigid plastic or metal. Egg and figure moulds were formerly made from copper with a silver lining. Moulds can be one-piece hollow figures, one half perhaps in polycarbonate, or two-piece moulds joined together with clips. In fact, any highly polished or shiny plastic mould is suitable, provided the moulded article can be removed without being damaged.

Prepare the mould by using cotton wool or a very soft cloth to polish the mould surface; the better the shine, the finer the moulded egg or figure will look. Well-tempered chocolate is also crucial to attaining a good finish.

Never wash moulds with any abrasive cleaners – only warm soapy water – and rinse well. Store moulds when not in use, wrapped in clingfilm or soft paper. Do not scratch the moulding surface: any damage or mark on the surface will be reproduced in the moulded object.

When the moulds are polished (which can take some time for high quality finishes) fill the mould with well-tempered couverture. Tap gently to remove any trapped air bubbles, which, if left, could spoil the figure or egg.

For egg halves, pour in tempered chocolate and swill round to cover the inside surface. Tip the mould over the bowl of couverture and allow excess chocolate to run off. Tap gently to remove any air pockets and clean the edge using a plastic scraper, never a metal blade. Place the coated half or single figure mould onto a clean surface of paper, preferably silicone, which can be re-used. The mould might require a second lining, but practice will develop the ability to coat with one good coat, saving time.

When the eggs have been moulded, leave them to set: never place them in a deep freeze as this will cause condensation to occur between the chocolate and the mould, spoiling the surface. Place the eggs in a fridge or near an open window. The chocolate will shrink away from the mould. Clear moulds develop a pearl opaque sheen when moulding has been successful. Any area of the mould that has not shrunk away from its surface will look wet. Slightly flexing the mould will allow the chocolate to shock away from the mould, to allow removal of the egg, shape or figure.

Moulded work made in two halves will need to be joined. Warm a flat tray and touch each half to melt the edge, then join the halves and leave to set. Alternatively, pipe each edge using liquid tempered couverture and join.

Moulded shapes can also be produced by

brushing the mould with chocolate to line the inside. This might require at least three coats to produce a good thickness of chocolate. Use a clean, dry, soft brush for this purpose.

Handle all moulded chocolate products with care. Often a fine finish is spoilt from the warmth of your fingers; use plastic gloves to prevent the surface being marked. Inquisitive onlookers will often investigate a finished mould by touching it – display moulded work can be varnished with confectioner's varnish to provide a high gloss and preserve the finish.

Moulded work can be decorated with piping chocolate, flowers made from sugar paste or marzipan, crystallised flowers or chocolate ribbons. Names or messages can be piped on with royal icing.

Egg moulds can be piped with couverture, using milk, white or plain or a mixture, to produce a lace egg which looks very impressive. Pipe each interior surface with a regular or irregular piped pattern and join while still wet, or join the separate halves when set. Pipe the edges with piping chocolate using a fancy small tube. Roses or other decorative flowers can be placed inside prior to joining to provide a special touch.

Piping

Moisture and steam can ruin chocolate as previously described, but the careful addition of specific ingredients can tighten the liquid chocolate, allowing the mixture to be piped. This will give a smooth and glossy finish to edge piping, torten and layer cakes, piped motifs, or any designs produced using royal icing.

Stir a small amount of the following ingredients into the warm liquid chocolate and continue until the mixture becomes thick; stir slowly to avoid trapping air, it can take a few minutes to thicken.

Spirit or liqueurs: These provide flavour and the chocolate retains its sheen.

Glycerine: Add a few drops per 250 g of liquid chocolate, stir well.

Piping jelly: This helps to retain sheen on the chocolate.

Stock syrup or fruit syrup: Syrup maintains the gloss on the chocolate and adds flavour.

Piped designs are limited only by your imagination. If they are piped directly onto squares of silicone or waxed paper, the set designs can be stored for future use. Make these when quiet as this skill is not easy to maintain under pressure. Baker's chocolate produces good results when used to highlight the design and decoration on cakes, pastries, fancies or for piping directly onto petits fours, pastilles or sweetmeats.

Pouring

Chocolate can be poured into templates or as a sheet and cut to produce an array of designs. Alternatively, shallow moulds can be used to pre-form shapes which can be used as decoration. Mat stencils can be made or purchased. The liquid chocolate is poured in and the tray or table agitated gently to remove any trapped air bubbles, or use a fine paint brush or cocktail stick for this purpose.

Sheet silicone or plastic can be covered with couverture and laid on a shape such as a ripple tray or corrugated plastic sheet to form unusual shapes or *pièce montée* work. This can be used with other chocolate products to enhance displays for buffets, receptions or special parties or banquets.

Plastic gloves can be filled with tempered couverture or baker's chocolate, securing the top with a bulldog clip. Hang the gloves to set.

These take some time to completely set and are best left overnight. Carefully remove the plastic glove to reveal a pair of hands. These can be mounted, holding a tray edged in lace piping for the presentation of chocolates or petits fours. Fingernails can be white on dark chocolate or dark on white chocolate. Any clean rubber mould used for plaster work can be used to pour chocolate to provide an unusual display for a shop window or buffet.

Modelling

Modelling or plastic chocolate is made by mixing one part warm glucose with two parts melted couverture or baker's chocolate at 32°C. The mixture takes a few minutes to blend and is prone to separating some of the cocoa butter fat. Remove the homogeneous mass and place in a clean plastic bag or bowl to set. This is ideal for modelling leaves, flowers, roses, baskets or as a sculpting medium. When a leaf has been formed, it can be polished with the palm of your hand or fingers to produce a bright sheen. Pin some modelling chocolate between clingfilm and use spring-loaded flower cutters to produce small flowers. These can be highlighted with white couverture; join with piping chocolate to make small dainty bouquets.

Carving

Chocolate is an excellent medium for the technique of carving: small sharp knives or blades and modelling tools are used to carve animals or figures.

This technique is not used today as it was 20 or 30 years ago, when large carved figures would grace the centre of buffets. For example, the pastry chef at Bournemouth and Poole College of Further Education used fine leather embellishment for his carved horse centre-pieces. Small bandages dipped in couverture

were used to form the base structure. The main layer was gradually built up, then the detail of muscles and folds was carved out of the animal form.

However, such elaborate designs are now seldom used except for a special banquet or competitive *pièce montée*. Chocolate carving is still used in Europe for small pieces such as fallow deer, small horses, unicorns, stags or bulls. Tempered chocolate can be poured into moulds and allowed to set and then carved to develop finer detail.

Dipping

To dip centres the equipment and centres need to be prepared and organised prior to dipping. Arrange the centres to be dipped in neat rows of equal number. Dipping by hand is a technique that requires practice to develop the finish and decoration seen in manufactured chocolates, although there are a growing number of small businesses providing a quality range of hand-dipped goods. The room temperature for dipping is important, just as the temperature of the centres is critical if a neat gloss finish is to be attained.

The best room working temperature for dipping is 18–19°C, while the cooling temperature if volume dipping is undertaken needs to be ideally 16–18°C. Avoid draughts, which can affect the final gloss on the dipped centres.

Take some tempered chocolate or covering chocolate which has a poorer taste for this type of work and ensure that the centres have a temperature of 29–30°C. Covering centres which are too warm or too cold will result in a dull finish or a grey bloom or streak. Cold centres will cause a dull finish on the chocolate; warm centres will create a sugar bloom as moisture vaporises and reacts with the sugar crystals.

Take three or four centres in your hand

Centres for dipping

Dipped chocolates

and drop them into the porringer of chocolate. Using a special dipping fork, raise and lower the centre into the couverture. Remove each centre and remove excess chocolate on the side of the pan, tapping lightly to achieve an even coating. Place the dipped centres on silicone paper in neat rows, starting at the far end of the paper and working towards you. The prongs of the fork are removed from the side of the centre not from the rear edge which causes a trail of chocolate. A rack needs to be available to store the dipped units until set or for further decoration.

COFFEE CARAMELS

Ingredients	
Double cream	570 ml
Granulated sugar	450 g
Glucose	225 g
Coffee powder	25 g

Boil and stir the ingredients to 140°C. Pour into oiled caramel bars. Cool and cut into shape. Dip in couverture and decorate.

MARZIPAN TORTA

Ingredients	
Lemon marzipan	200 g
Orange marzipan	200 g
Apricot marzipan	200 g
Pistachio marzipan	200 g
Coffee marzipan	200 g

Roll each piece of marzipan to a thickness of 4 mm. Layer the colours and press between marzipan bars. Cut out 20 mm circles and dry for 2 hours. Dip in couverture and decorate.

CHOCOLATE FUDGE CUBES

Ingredients	
Double cream	300 ml
Butter	225 g
Honey or glucose	225 g
Granulated sugar	900 g
Couverture	250 g

Cook the ingredients in a large pan to 120°C, stirring continuously. Take care not to burn the base of the mixture. Pour into oiled sugar bars or tray. Cool, and cut into 25 mm cubes. Dip and decorate.

TURKISH DELIGHT

Ingredients	
Sugar	2.5 kg
Arrowroot	250 g
Glucose or honey	125 g
Rose or orange flower water	1 litre
Leaf gelatine	125 g
Icing sugar	300 g
Powdered magnesia	50 g

Dissolve the starch in 250 ml water. Boil the sugar, glucose/honey to 120°C. Add the starch and cook until the mixture thickens. Add the soaked gelatine and strain. Pour the mixture into a wet tray to set. Remove from tray when set. Cut and powder using icing sugar and magnesia, or lightly dust with icing sugar when cut. Shake off any surplus. Dry for 1 hour – dip into couverture.

GANACHE BOULE

Ingredients	
Double cream	750 g
Plain/milk couverture	1.5 kg
Brandy, rum or kirsch to flavour	

Boil the cream. Add and stir in the chopped couverture. When set, roll into balls. Either dust with cocoa powder and place in petit four cases or dip into couverture and roll with a fork while setting on silicone paper to produce a spiked finish.

WHITE GIANDUJA CREAM BOULE

Ingredients	
Ground roasted almonds	250 g
Ground roasted hazelnuts	250 g
Icing sugar	500 g
White chocolate	250 g

Mix the nuts and sugar well. Add the chocolate and blend. Mix slowly to a smooth paste. Form into balls and dip into white or dark couverture. Finish by whipping with dark piping for white or white piping for dark Gianduja boules.

PEPPERMINT CREAMS

Ingredients

Fondant	1 kg
Peppermint oil or flavouring	
Apple green colouring	

Warm the fondant without water to 125°C. Stir in colour and peppermint to flavour. Pipe/funnel onto starch tray or silicone paper and allow to set. Using a dipping fork, dip each mint into couverture. Decorate the top with a three-prong dipping fork just before the couverture sets.

MILK PRALINE DELIGHT

Ingredients

Fine praline powder	400 g
Milk couverture	600 g
Vanilla	

Make praline from roasted hazelnuts. Melt the couverture and stir in the praline; mix well and pipe the mixture into pre-formed small chocolate cups or directly onto silicone paper to set. Decorate with a sugared hazelnut or crystallised flowers.

TRUFFLES – WHITE, DARK AND MILK

Ingredients

White, milk or plain couverture	600 g
Double cream	450 ml
Toasted ground almonds	250 g
Brandy	100 ml
Fine sponge crumbs	100 g

Boil the cream, then stir in the chopped chocolate. Add brandy and stir well. Mix in the almonds and sponge crumbs, then pipe or roché into 15 g pieces. Form into balls when set, and dip carefully into tempered chocolate. As the truffles set, roll with a fine fork to ripple the surface of the chocolate. Alternatively, the truffles can be dusted with cocoa powder and dusted with icing sugar from a muslin pouch. The truffles can be rolled, when initially moulded, in vermicelli or roasted nibbed almonds or pistachio.

The basic truffle recipe found in many recipe books can be used as a filling, coating or for piping decoration such as Truffle Torte. Adjust the ratio of chocolate to cream to alter the firmness of the mixture. Butter can be blended with couverture to produce a truffle buttercream as in the following recipe.

CURAÇAO BUTTER TRUFFLE MIX

Ingredients

Unsalted butter	400 g
Curaçao	150 ml
Brandy	50 ml
Couverture or baker's chocolate	1 kg
Italian meringue	400 g

Make the meringue and beat until cool. Cream the butter, curaçao and brandy. Pour in the melted chocolate and beat well. Blend in the meringue. Place in a bowl and cover. Use as required.

COINTREAU MARZIPAN LOGS

Ingredients

Marzipan	700 g
Cointreau	100 ml
Icing sugar	175 g
Liquid glucose	25 g

Blend the ingredients and leave to stand for 24 hours. Divide the mixture into 3 equal portions and roll to form ropes, approximately 10 mm thick. Place two of the ropes together with the third on top; these could be coloured

Steps to making cointreau marzipan logs

differently for contrast. Cut into manageable 20 cm lengths. Brush with melted chocolate and leave to set. When firm, turn the log and brush the base surface until a coating of chocolate surrounds the length. Cut into 2 cm pieces and decorate with white piping chocolate.

Cocoa painting

The art of cocoa painting, once widely used to highlight gâteaux and tortes, as a decorative picture for plaques and eggs or as the main *pièce montée* display on a major chocolate centrepiece, has largely vanished. Few artists now use this technique, although it is a useful and subtle technique to enhance the appeal of chocolate fare. Work in a natural light if possible or a well-lit room. Cocoa painting is effective when darker shades and soft lines of a picture, landscape, animal or figure are painted onto a white chocolate plaque or egg.

TOOLS AND WORKING MATERIALS REQUIRED

You will need a selection of fine paintbrushes, artist's tracing paper, soft pencil, chocolate plaque, marzipan, royal icing, pastillage or sugar paste, cocoa powder, cocoa butter, oil, a small sharp knife and a cloth to wipe your brushes with.

Select a picture to copy and trace it using the tracing paper and soft pencil. Lay the tracing paper over the image and lightly trace the outline of the picture. Remove the tracing paper, turn it over, and outline the image on the opposite side of the tracing paper. Place the tracing in the correct position on the plaque or surface to receive the painting.

Lightly re-trace with a pencil to transfer the outline of the image onto the plaque surface. This can be done by gently rubbing the tracing to print the image as a guide for the cocoa paint. Alternatively, the cocoa powder can be mixed with a small amount of water and painted onto the rear of the tracing. This must be left to dry completely and then placed into position on the plaque surface. Gently re-trace the pencil lines to transfer the cocoa film onto the surface of the plaque. Finish shading and filling the painting using light and dark cocoa mixes.

PREPARING THE COCOA PAINT

Mix one part cocoa butter with two parts oil. Lightly warm this and add the cocoa powder to the desired shade; mix to a smooth consistency. This mixture can be thinned using cocoa butter or oil, but when used needs to be kept warm. Place the paint in a small clean tray or dish over a night light held in a jar; leave a space for oxygen to feed the flame. Use

Cocoa painting

the paint to outline the tracing. Thinned paint can be used to shade areas for light or dark shadow; darker shades can be achieved by adding more cocoa powder.

Select simple images to paint; these will give practice before attempting more complex landscape or portrait tasks. Portraits are the most difficult as slight variations in shadow, filling or line will portray a different effect.

TIPS FOR PAINTING WITH COCOA PAINT

1   Start in the centre of the outline and work to the edges.
2   Use a light shade of cocoa paint to begin, it can be darkened later.
3   Small fine brushes are more useful for cocoa painting.
4   Test the cocoa mix on a piece of white base first to judge the shade.

5 Select simple images to copy when beginning.
6 Keep the cocoa butter mixture warm over a night light in a jar.
7 Allow fine line work to dry before filling or shading.
8 Paint the deeper shades of a picture first, then move to the lighter shading.

Cocoa painting can be enjoyable and frames of chocolate using a mixture of techniques can produce an eye-catching piece. White chocolate Easter eggs look special when painted with an Easter bunny.

Spraying and nappé

Chocolate spraying is not a technique used by the everyday artist. Special equipment is needed to spray the thinned chocolate, but the effect and finish is indeed different. Figures and centres can be sprayed to produce a quite different surface than dipping or nappé techniques. Few centres in this country use this method – it is more popular in Germany, Austria, Switzerland and Belgium. Equipment can be purchased for as little as £200.

Nappé means coated. Ganache mixtures or chocolate can be used to cover small or large items to produce a smooth finish. Confidence is required to ensure larger tortes are covered completely with no bubbles or marks.

The recipe used and the working temperature will affect the technique of nappé. Use a large ladle for bigger goods and a smaller ladle for small goods. Ganache should be used soon after production to produce a clean even finish and a fine gloss or mirror surface. If difficulties are experienced then adjust the chocolate content: less if too thick, more if too thin. Practise and note the adjustments to your recipe for future reference. As soon as you cover a product, remove air bubbles with a cocktail stick or fine dry paintbrush. When preparing any mixture for nappé, stir slowly to avoid aerating the mixture.

Runouts

Just as with royal icing (page 54), chocolate is a good medium for producing runouts. Using a piping chocolate for the frame and a liquid chocolate and piping bag, runouts of varying shapes and designs can be produced.

Use a mixture of chocolates to produce a very effective mottled filling. Individual designs repeated can be used to enhance gâteau and torte items or as a garnish for desserts and small confectionery.

Ribbons and bows

Take a flexible plastic sheet (the best for this purpose is an overhead transparency) and cut it into 2.5 cm widths. Using a small palette knife, spread some well-tempered plain couverture over a strip, serrate with a comb scraper along the length and allow to set. Next take some white couverture, spread thinly over the strip of chocolate and plastic, and leave to set. Finally, spread with dark chocolate, and fold the strip immediately to form a bow. Set in the fridge, then carefully peel off the plastic to reveal a shiny two-tone ribbonette. Join a number of these to form a full bow, finishing with a selection of chocolate flowers made from plastic chocolate or marzipan.

CHOCOLATE PRODUCTS

Decorations

Many items can be produced in chocolate and stored until required for use. The designs should be pleasant to the eye, balanced and of

Piped template and runout design

Steps to making chocolate bows

the same size. The following list gives some of the types of decoration that can be produced or purchased easily.

Coffee beans
Piping designs
Copeaux
Vermicelli
Cut-outs
Truffles
Shavings
Grated chocolate
Boules

CHOCOLATE COFFEE BEANS
These can be made from modelling chocolate, formed into a small oval shape in the hands and marked with the back of a knife.

TRUFFLES
Make up a truffle cream and, when cool, produce small truffles for decoration on gâteaux and tortes. These can be rolled in liquid couverture, cocoa powder or chocolate vermicelli.

PIPING DESIGNS
Piping designs can be produced with a piping chocolate as described on page 128. Pipe directly onto silicone sheets, allow these to set and store in a cool clean place until required for decoration.

SHAVINGS
Either shave from a solid block of chocolate, from a hand grater or use a plain cutter to draw across set couverture on a marble slab. Store and use as required.

COPEAUX AU CHOCOLAT
Thinly spread some melted couverture, working it back and forwards. When this sets, use the tilted blade of a scraper or knife – this should be held at a 30° angle – to push the chocolate away from you, lifting the angle of the knife as you cut to 90°. The higher the cutting angle, the smaller the cigarette (*copeau*) produced. Store in a cool place until required for decoration of cold desserts, gâteaux, tortes, tea fancies and confectionery.

GRATED CHOCOLATE
Chocolate can be grated from the block onto silicone paper and kept cool. Use as an edging decoration for gâteaux, trifles, or cold dessert items.

VERMICELLI
Vermicelli is purchased in white, dark or milk forms; if old they will discolour. Empty a quantity onto a tray and use. If using for edging a gâteau, for example, then make certain no residual cream or butter cream is placed back in with the stock of this item; this can cause cross-contamination and become a problem. If a plain cutter is pressed through a cardboard template, this can be positioned in the centre of a torte and the vermicelli poured into it to produce a neat ring centre. Carefully lift the card template and cutter off.

BOULES
Modelling chocolate or truffle mixtures can be formed into balls and dipped as a decoration, dusted with a pouch of icing sugar or topped with crystallised mimosa flowers. Positioned around a *Torte au chocolat*, they provide a simple but effective presentation.

CUT-OUTS
Tempered couverture or baker's chocolate can be poured and set; templates or cutters can then be used to cut out shapes for a decoration item. Animal or leaf shapes of metal can be used; warm the cutter carefully and press onto the set chocolate. Plaques can be cut with an oval fluted cutter; these can then be cut again with an animal template and filled with white

chocolate on a plain background. Highlight with cocoa paint for a neat finish.

Sauces and fillings

HAZELNUT AND CHOCOLATE BUTTERCREAM

Ingredients	
Egg	600 g
Caster sugar	300 g
Butter	525 g
Chocolate	300 g
Ground hazelnuts	300 g

Whisk the sugar and eggs to a sponge. When cool, beat in the butter. Add the melted chocolate. Add the hazelnuts and beat well. Store and use as required.

CHOCOLATE PRALINE BUTTERCREAM

Ingredients	
Butter	500 g
Italian meringue	500 g
Chocolate	300 g
Almond praline	100 g

Beat the butter well. When cool beat in the meringue. Add the chocolate and praline. Store and use as required.

CHOCOLATE ARRACK BUTTERCREAM

Ingredients	
Buttercream	600 g
Chocolate	100 g
Arrack	60 ml

Beat the butter well. Add the chocolate and arrack. Store and use as required.

HAZELNUT CHOCOLATE BUTTERCREAM

Ingredients	
White chocolate	500 g
Gianduya	200 g
Rum	150 ml
Hazelnut praline	200 g
Butter	200 g

Beat the butter, praline and rum well. Add the chocolate and gianduya. Beat well and place in clean bowl. Store and use as required. Rum can be replaced with brandy or kirsch.

CHOCOLATE CREAM

Ingredients	
Butter	600 g
Gianduya	600 g
White chocolate	1 kg
Boiled milk	300 ml

Beat the chocolate and gianduya. Add the boiled milk slowly and mix. Beat well and cool. Store for 24 hours, then beat in the previously softened butter. Store and use as required.

CHOCOLATE CUSTARD

Ingredients	
Milk	550 ml
Cream	225 ml
Arrowroot	28 g
Sugar	200 g
Egg yolk	125 g
Couverture	100 g
Vanilla essence	

Dissolve the arrowroot in a little milk. Boil the milk, cream and sugar. Add the arrowroot. Pour onto the well-beaten egg yolk and cook for 2 minutes. Pour onto the chocolate, a little at a time. Blend and flavour with vanilla.

CHOCOLATE ICING – SOFT

Ingredients	
Water	1.1 litre
Glucose	100 g
Granulated sugar	1.36 kg
Couverture	300 g
Leaf gelatine	28 g

Boil the sugar, glucose and water. Add the soaked gelatine. Melt the couverture to 37°C, then add to the syrup until the correct consistency is attained.

Chocolate mousse – white, milk or plain

The following basic recipe can be used to produce a quality mousse as a dessert or base of a more elaborate sweet.

Ingredients	
Fresh double or whipping cream	500 ml
Couverture or baker's chocolate	150 g
Egg white	4
Cube sugar	225 g

Whip the cream lightly and place in the fridge. Melt the chocolate. Produce an Italian meringue from the egg whites and sugar, taking care not to 'grain' the meringue. Carefully combine the cream and chocolate and, when half mixed, fold in the meringue (fold until clear). Care needs to be taken when folding in at each stage or the volume of the mixture will be lost. Pipe into glasses and chill in the fridge for at least one hour. Decorate with a chocolate piped motif or chocolate shavings. Dust with a mixture of cocoa powder and icing sugar.

Ganache – white, milk or plain

Ganache is a mixture of cream and chocolate. The cream is boiled and the finely chopped or grated chocolate is stirred in until a smooth, high-gloss mixture results. Ganache has a wide variety of uses; it can be used whilst warm to coat individual cakes and pastries, for log or bar cakes, and as a neat quality coating for gateaux and torten. Ganache is a good base for truffles which can be mixed with toasted nibbed or ground nuts, fruit and liqueurs. Fillings made from a mixture of unsalted butter and ganache are useful for cakes, pastries, gateaux and torte products.

RECIPE 1

Ingredients	
Fresh double cream	570 ml
Couverture or baker's chocolate	1.4 kg
Vanilla pod or essence	
Butter	110 g

Boil the cream and vanilla. Remove from the stove and stir in the chopped or grated chocolate. Stir well and add to the softened butter. Mix to a clear, high-gloss mixture. The mix may curdle initially, but keep mixing until the ganache amalgamates to form a clear, smooth, soft texture. For covering, the ganache is used at this stage (that is while still warm). Any other ingredients such as glacé fruit, nuts or sultanas and raisins can also be added at this stage. When cool, the mix is formed into truffles.

The mixture can be poured and spread on a tray lined with silicone paper, cooled in the fridge overnight and then demoulded and cut into shapes for petits fours. The slab of set ganache can be decorated with chocolate piping and cut into pieces.

RECIPE 2

Ingredients

Fresh double cream	400 ml
Couverture or baker's chocolate	1.2 kg
Butter (soft)	600 g
Kirsch, rum, cointreau, Grand Marnier, and Tia Maria can be used individually	

Proceed as for recipe 1. Form the mixture into ball (*boule*) shapes, either by using two teaspoons or by piping using a savoy bag and plain tube. Place the balls onto silicone paper sheets in neat rows. Chill the shapes until firm (2 hours). The truffles can be dipped quickly into tempered couverture and rolled in cocoa powder, or rolled using a dipping fork on the silicone paper to form a spiked surface. Dipping into couverture must be done quickly or the boule will begin to melt. A set of dipping forks will be useful for this purpose.

Flavoured coating

There are now a wide range of flavoured chocolate-based coatings for the confectioner, baker or pastry chef to use. Companies such as Ritter-Couriveaud can supply specialist mixtures for a complete range of uses, as coatings, piping mediums or fillings. Fudge-based coatings which can be heated and used like fondant can be purchased and produce good results. Coloured chocolate is available in blue and orange for novelty work and colour contrast. Fondant can also be flavoured and coloured to coat chocolate or marzipan, fudge, fruit or nut centres.

6 FURTHER INFORMATION FOR THE PROFESSIONAL CHEF

■ DISPLAY

Display is important to any business, whether a large or small company or a manufacturer. It is an essential part of sales promotion which no business can afford to neglect because of the advantages it has to offer.

Retail display embraces most areas of the shop, including windows, refrigerated counters, cold buffets for wedding receptions, conferences, dinner dances, etc.

The objectives of display

While some enlightened confectioners have realised the value of good displays, many still dress their windows in a style which was fashionable three or four generations ago. Such windows inform passers-by what the shop is, but go no further than this. Windows are often overcrowded and lack any intelligent analysis of the selling qualities of the products offered for sale. Display is the best medium for advertising, as it puts over the sales message, backed up with a visual presentation of the merchandise. This is the strongest link between retailer and consumer, and those creating the display shoulder a great responsibility for the selling process.

The objective of a display is to attract the customer, give a favourable impression and by so doing increase sales. The main purpose is to create sales that might otherwise not have occurred; to make sales through impulse, increase casual sales and those which might otherwise have gone to competitors. Good displays establish contact with potential customers while still catering for the needs of the existing ones. Display reflects the character of the establishment, helps to publicise the services offered and builds up goodwill.

Since the introduction of mass-production, many shops carry identical merchandise, so more thought needs to be given to the presentation of such goods. The smaller business has no such problems, being able to establish and maintain its own character and identity through the varied selection it has to offer.

Preparing the display area

It is normal practice for confectioners or pâtissiers to display their efforts from a central position: a cold buffet at the entrance to attract the eye of the arriving guests or visitors or, for the bakery shop, a display that can be seen from a central position on the pavement.

The display has to catch the customers' attention when they are not intentionally looking at it; it will be particularly effective when the view comes as a surprise. Catch the customers' attention with goods placed in the path of the line of vision; tall, artistic centrepieces need to be displayed at the back of the produce, so that the arrangement cascades towards the front.

Avoid overcrowding as it bewilders the visitors or passers-by; it is essential to eliminate unnecessary clutter. The display has to be artistic and pleasing to the eye. The following design principles should be considered:

1 Preparation
2 Space
3 Lay-out
4 Design
5 Quantity
6 Colour
7 Lighting

Good design is the essence of display; without it, no display can accomplish its purpose. If you are preparing a display in a restaurant, the size and shape of the room has to be considered. Design creates the audience, holds their attention and links together all the elements that make up a promotion.

REQUIREMENTS FOR THE COLD BUFFET

1 Correct positioning of the tables and tablecloths.
2 Space for visitors to walk freely round, avoiding congestion and disturbing the display.
3 Ensure all dishes are set in the appropriate position, facing the front of the displays. Arrange the dishes to a pre-planned design, not merely putting them on the table. The setting must suggest pleasure for the prospective customer, and be pleasing to the eye.
4 The quantity of dishes displayed varies according to the number of guests attending; only a certain number can be displayed at one go – the rest can be brought out at a later stage. Each dish should supply 6–12 portions. Individual dishes are not suitable to display on the cold buffet table.
5 The food presented is made with the intention of being eaten; it should be appealing and appetising.
6 The table should not be situated in a dark corner of the restaurant. Lighting is a priority consideration – if not correctly planned

it can distort the design and colour of the work done. Lighting should enhance the presentation of the food and the work of the centrepieces.

Remember
1 Attract attention
2 Maintain attention
3 Arouse interest
4 Welcome the visitors

■ HYGIENE AND FOOD SAFETY

Maintaining a professional standard at all times and in all situations is at the heart of professional competence. You need to look not only at the individual elements, but also at the complete process of presentation and service. Poor dress, presentation and standards of hygiene undermine the professional status of an organisation and reflect on individuals as part of that business; the net result is that business is adversely affected.

The risk of contamination over recent years has become focused with the reporting of many cases where poor standards of food hygiene and handling procedures resulted in customers and staff needing medical attention. We all have a duty to be clean and to prevent contamination by careful handling and storage of food materials from delivery to the finished product or service.

Every person involved with the handling, preparation and production of food has a duty to be clean and to pay due attention to bad habits. Employers are bound under the health and safety regulations to provide or ensure protective clothing is worn and the appropriate cleaning materials are available to maintain a professional and hygienic environment.

Food hygiene regulations state that protective clothing should be worn when handling food. Employers supply and launder these garments, or employees purchase their own protective clothing and usually the employer meets the cleaning costs. It is essential to keep all protective clothing in good clean order, regularly washed – daily if in food preparation areas. Kitchen staff sometimes go out to the shops or wear their whites in town or in public: this needs to be discouraged as it is where contamination is likely to occur. Protective clothing should be worn for the purpose it is intended. A chef that wears dirty whites, no necktie or apron, and the top button undone projects a very unprofessional image which must not be tolerated.

Protective clothing

1. Protects from hot liquids in the case of a chef's jacket.
2. Prevents contamination from personal clothing and other contact from pets.
3. Prevents contamination: a loose button can fall into food.
4. Needs to be in good repair to prevent injury from machinery.
5. Should be kept clean and changed at regular intervals; food stains and soiled aprons and jackets harbour bacteria which result in contamination.
6. Shoes need particular attention: wear safety shoes and avoid wearing pumps – these make your feet sweat and contribute to 'athlete's foot'.
7. Keep your feet clean, changing socks regularly. Powder can prevent 'athlete's foot' occurring.
8. Wear a necktie in the kitchen to absorb perspiration.
9. Never wear your everyday clothing under protective clothing.
10. Be clean, smart and professional at all times.

Bacteria

The optimum temperature for the growth of food poisoning organisms is 37°C (body temperature). The further away from this temperature, the slower the growth. To slow the growth of bacteria, foods should be kept out of the temperature range of 5–63°C, often called the *danger zone*.

Temperatures below freezing point do not kill bacteria, therefore any chilled or thawed food needs careful handling and should be treated in exactly the same way as for fresh food. Above 63°C, bacteria vary in their response. Most will be killed, but some are able to produce spores to enable them to survive. These spores can survive up to five hours in boiling water.

■ PACKAGING AND LABELLING

If food items are sold packaged, then the ingredients should be displayed with the nutritional information (where applicable) on a label. This information is important and needs to be carefully studied to ensure you meet with current food labelling regulations.

The law ensures that labels provide 'factual information' about the product, which means you are not allowed to present information about the food item that is not fact, such as 'reduced calorie'.

1. Ingredients should be listed in order of weight and include any additives used in the composition of the product.
2. Additives listed in the ingredients should state what their function is with the relevant name or 'E' number.
3. If flavourings are used then this must be stated on the label but they do not need to be named.

4 Nutritional information can be provided but is not mandatory.

5 A datemark must appear on the product.

6 Instructions for safe storage should be provided.

7 The name and address of the producer or manufacturer should be provided.

8 A large **e** following the weight indicates that the average quantity must be accurate, but that the weight of each pack may vary slightly.

9 The name of the product on the label must not be misleading and should state if the food item has been processed.

10 Food that is sold unwrapped does not need to carry a label, but a ticket or notice needs to be provided showing its proper name and the type of any additives, e.g. 'contains preservatives'.

Best before and use by

1 A *Use by* datemark indicates the date by which highly perishable foods should be used. Food should be labelled clearly with the term *Use by*, followed by the date.

2 A *Best Before* datemark indicates the date up to and including which the manufacturer or retailer anticipates the food item to remain at peak quality, as long as it has been stored correctly. Longer life food items can label the food item with *Best Before End*, followed by the date.

The datemark on food labels must be in a prominent position, or there should be clear advice where to find the datemark.

Sell by terms have been phased out with the exception of eggs.

If you are in any doubt as to your legal obligations when packaging and labelling food items, always consult your local trading standards office.

■ SERVICING EQUIPMENT AND SERVICE CONTRACTS

Apart from labour costs, the capital equipment costs in setting up a catering business and service costs and repairs during the working life of your equipment are the most costly outlay. It is easy to allow service contracts to end in the hope that money is saved and that machines will continue to operate. The general experience, however, is that when you end a service contract sooner rather than later, machines break down or parts fail, resulting in a loss of revenue while engineers attend to the work. The call-out charges and repair costs also tend to be greater if machinery is allowed to fall into disrepair.

Always ensure a reputable contractor deals with your equipment. Managers and employers do need to ensure economies are made when contracts are agreed, to get the best support in the shortest time at the minimum cost. Some services which are provided might be the cheapest, but are not always the most effective or efficient.

Regular servicing of all major equipment is an investment in the business. Where large or complicated equipment is concerned, the manufacturer is often the best contractor to supply support and regular maintenance. Bakeries have call-out contracts where engineers will respond quickly to prevent production losses; this type of insurance is essential for modern process catering.

Always ensure, when agreeing contracts, that your solicitor has been through the papers in detail and that you understand the implications in signing and also the limitations agreed. Ensure extra costs are clearly stated by the contractor before any contract is agreed.

Regular cleaning and basic care of any piece of equipment will prolong its working life and extend the initial and ongoing investment in service contracts. Catering businesses tend to ignore such regular maintenance, only acting when a key machine item packs up or fails completely.

The three most common faults with machinery tend to be:

1 *Electrical failure:* An element, wire or connection breaks, shorts or burns out.
2 *Mechanical failure:* A gear or load-bearing/friction-bearing part wears out and needs replacing.
3 *Human error*: The machine is over-loaded, not used correctly according to manufacturers instructions, not set up correctly or pieces of the machine are not assembled correctly after cleaning.

When using specialist equipment, ensure staff are familiar with its use, cleaning and operation. Basic oiling with mineral oil is often overlooked; know how to oil basic parts. Check that attachments are fitted correctly each time the machine is re-assembled. Provide notices to make certain safety procedures are followed when using dangerous machines, such as slicers, mincers, fryers, dividers and moulders.

QUESTIONS

■ PRODUCE PASTILLAGE, MARZIPAN, CHOCOLATE AND SUGAR PRODUCTS

Prepare and use pastillage, marzipan and decorative icings

		Page reference
1	Give a definition of pastillage.	76
2	Name two different agents used for setting pastillage.	76
3	What is tragacanth?	76
4	Describe the main uses for pastillage.	79
5	From what substance does gelatine originate?	76
6	What should the texture and condition of the pastillage be like before rolling or moulding?	77–8
7	Give the advantages and disadvantages of using tragacanth to make pastillage.	77–8
8	Give the advantages and disadvantages of using gelatine to make pastillage.	77–8
9	Describe the precautions necessary during the production of pastillage to ensure the paste is smooth and pliable and doesn't stick.	78–9
10	How is colour best incorporated into the pastillage?	83
11	When rolling out pastillage, what would be a suitable thickness?	79
12	Describe the correct condition of rolled-out pastillage.	79
13	What would happen if the pieces of cut pastillage were too thick and unevenly rolled out?	79
14	How are the cut pieces stored for drying?	80
15	Describe the method for assembling the cut pieces.	81
16	What steps should be taken to minimise the amount of leftovers and trimmings. How are they stored?	79–80
17	What can be added to pastillage to facilitate the production of flowers?	89
18	Sketch/design a pencil for a pastillage centrepiece.	84–5
19	Draw a 15 cm round pastillage plaque or plate to be used on the top of a cake for a special occasion. Identify the decorations, inscriptions and colours used.	84–5
20	Describe briefly what is meant by each of the following: (a) Primary colours (b) Secondary colours (c) Tertiary colours	8
21	Maintaining cleanliness in the preparation and production of confectionery products is essential. Explain why preparation areas and equipment need to be kept clean throughout production.	14, 95, 96, 100, 104, 114, 127, 129, 142–4

22   State the conditions suitable for the storage of marzipan commodities and products.

23   What factors influence the quality of marzipan products? Describe the influence of each on achieving the correct:
(a) Texture
(b) Appearance
(c) Consistency

Prepare, process and finish chocolate coatings and couverture-based products

		Page reference

1   Describe in detail the preparation of chocolate for tempering using the followng methods: 123–5
(a) Slab method
(b) Cooling method
(c) Seeding method

2   Discuss the stages of preparation of equipment and ingredients when producing moulded chocolate figures, eggs or shapes. Describe the production stages in moulding and the precautions to be considered in ensuring a good quality finish.   127–8

3   Piping chocolate can be prepared by adding any one of a range of thickening agents. List three liquids suitable for thickening chocolate for piping.   128

4   Sketch 12 different designs suitable for piping as a motif.   128

5   Sketch six different centres which would be suitable for dipping in chocolate. Describe the preparation and production of any three of these centres and give a detailed description of the dipping procedure.   57–75, 129–33

6   State the optimum temperature of centres prior to dipping.   129

7   List the main recipe ingredients for the following chocolates: 123, 126
(a) Plain couverture
(b) Milk couverture
(c) White chocolate
Give the working temperatures for each chocolate.

8   How are chocolate and chocolate products best stored to keep them in premium condition? Which common faults can occur if the storage conditions deteriorate?   121

9   What needs to be checked before a chocolate shape is removed from a mould?   127

10   Describe when and why an enrober might be used in chocolate production.   125

11   Explain why baker's chocolate can be cut more readily than couverture.   137

12   How are *coupeax au chocolat* made? Why is 'spreading' an important technique in their production?   137

13   Describe the technique of cocoa painting. Suggest a range of items that might use this method of decoration, and sketch a cameo drawing of your choice.   133–5

Process and finish sugar-based products

		Page reference

1   State the grades of sugars suitable for producing a sugar solution.   3–5

2   Describe how sugar may be treated to produce a non-crystalline substance.   12

3   What proportion of water should be added to sugar to produce a saturated solution?   12

4   Why is liquid glucose added to the sugar solution? What effect will it have on the boiled solution?   13–14

5   What other substance could be added to the sugar solution instead of glucose?   13

6   Explain what is meant by crystallisation.   13

7   How does the addition of glucose or acid help to prevent crystallisation?   17

8   Describe in full three or four other precautions that help to prevent crystals forming.   12–13

9   Describe the procedure for testing sugar degrees without the aid of a sugar boiling thermometer.   16

10   What do the following terms mean?   16
(a) Soft ball
(b) Hard ball
(c) Soft crack
(d) Crack

11   What is rock sugar?   26–7

12   Why is it important to maintan the temperature of fondant below 38°C for dipping   28

13   List the utensils required for boiling and pulling sugar.   32

14   Briefly describe the sugar pulling process.   32–4

15   Describe the appearance of a poured sugar centrepiece, where calcium carbonate has been added to the solution.   22

16   At what stage and under what conditions should calcium carbonate be added when cooking sugar for poured sugar work?   22

17   What are the causes of recrystallisation of the sugar solution when dipping fruit déguisés?   65–6

18   Why might fruits weep when dipped in boiled sugar?   63–4

19   Explain why the boiling of the honey affects the quality of nougat montelimar.   71

20   Nougat montelimar and marshmallow contain egg. In each case, explain how bacterial growth is prevented.   71–2

21   Describe how a saccharometer is used to test degrees *Baumé* in the production of fruits confits.   68

22   What is the temperature of the cooked sugar in the production of each of the following:
(a) Spun sugar   25
(b) Rock sugar   26
(c) Fruits confits   67–8
(d) Nougat montelimar   71

23   Using 1 kg sugar, list the utensils, ingredients and method used in the production of one batch of:
(a) Dipped oranges and grapes   63–4
(b) Hard caramels   69
(c) Berlingots   70–1
(d) Croquantes   72–4
(e) Croquante centrepiece   72–5

24   Describe how you would present a finished centrepiece on a cold buffet table, made from either pulled sugar or croquante and surrounded, for example, with friandises, petits fours and gateaux. You may want to use a sketch to illustrate your answer.   141